"Whoa! Damn it, whoa!"

N IS FOR KNUCKLEHEADS

Bad Decisions
Facts vs Beliefs, and
America's Deference to Ignorance

by

JOE GENSHLEA

August 2015

DOCKSIDE SAILING PRESS®

Newport Beach, California

Dockside Sailing Press
Craig B. Smith, editor
Newport Beach, California
www.docksidesailingpress.com
123

Cover illustration by George Price ©*Condé Nast*
Used with permission.

Author's Dedication

Dedicated to Charles Darwin, who put
up with a lot of KNUCKLEHEADS

**Darwin Awards commemorate those
who improve our gene pool by
removing themselves from it.**

Editor's Note

In the United States today there is a growing concern that "Government is Broken." Much of the blame falls on Congress. In the last several years we have seen internal bickering in Congress cause the United States to fail to pass a budget in a timely manner, bringing about a government shutdown, resulting in its credit rating being lowered; to see numerous votes (all useless, since it was known in advance that they would not pass) to shut down the Affordable Care Act, which Congress previously approved, and other equally meaningless gestures. Our elected representatives, all receiving high salaries, sit in their fancy Washington offices and ***do not conduct*** the people's business.

Much is spoken or written about "Constitutional Rights," but the conclusions drawn are so far off base that one wonders if these elected representatives have ever bothered to read the Constitution.

Equally dismaying are decisions handed down by the Supreme Court, which seems to be ruling based on its view of politics rather than a neutral but strict interpretation of the law.

Congress has become ineffective: no compromise, so nothing gets done. For example, we all know that the United States is a nation of immigrants. Yet, like many other pressing concerns facing the nation, Congress refuses to deal with the immigration issue.

Joe Genshlea has written a brilliant summary of where we are and how we got to this place where the "Government is Broken." You will find it fascinating.

-Craig B. Smith, Editor
Balboa, CA.
August 2015

Contents

Author's Foreword (Or Why I Wrote This Book)

As a long-time trial lawyer, over the years I have been asked about what goes into winning a complicated legal case. My response has always been the same: good facts.

It is analogous to winning a football game. Bill Walsh was a great coach, but the *fact* that the San Francisco Forty-Niners had Joe Montana and Jerry Rice on the team made a big *difference*.

The point is, good lawyers always check and double check and drill down on all the facts before they go to trial. That has made me particularly curious about the factual basis of much of what passes for the truth as recited over and over again by politicians on both the right and the left and by the popular media.

Do you know what the "N" on your gear shift means? When can you call someone a liar? After 27 amendments, what's left of the original Constitution? How did the 13 states go about corralling the new Federal Government? Why were there no fatalities from the Fukushima nuclear plant meltdown? How is the military draft connected to Saint Augustine's just war? Is the Supreme Court just another political arm of the government? Is America a democracy? How wrong were Justice Scalia's decisions in the Right to Bear Arms cases?

These and other questions have bothered me for a long time, and so I have, in this book, attempted to take a closer look and give you my thoughts about the facts as I see them. I think many of my answers will surprise you.

You may even agree with me.

Joe Genshlea
Sacramento, CA

Chapter 1

"N" is for Knuckleheads
(Or America's Deference to Ignorance)

I suspect each generation believes it has seen extraordinary changes during its time. It seems to be particularly true during my lifetime. I was born in 1938 and the explosion of knowledge since then is staggering. The medicine practiced in the 1930s is closer to the Middle Ages than it is to the medicine practiced today. Nearly every discipline we study has been revolutionized. Psychiatry: psychotropic drugs; Astronomy: deep space telescopes and space travel; Physics: subatomic particles, the Higgs Boson and the Large Hadron Collider; Communications: the development of the semiconductor, the transistor, the computer, the internet, the smart phone and the information age; Travel: advent of the jumbo jet and automobiles that are operated by computers. It can all be quite overwhelming.

This huge explosion of knowledge brought back a dim memory. I was told somewhere in my youth that the last person who could credibly claim to know all that was then to be known was Francis Bacon. I did a little checking. Will and Ariel Durant in their volume on *The Age of Reason Begins*, call Bacon "The greatest and proudest intellect of the age."[1] They call his *Novum Organum* (1620) "The most brilliant production in English philosophy, the first clear call for an Age of Reason."[2] Jacques Barzun writes that, "By the mid-18th Century, the Age of Reason, Bacon was what Aristotle had been for so long, the master of those who know."[3] And Immanuel Kant dedicated his *Critique of Pure Reason* to Bacon. Pretty heady stuff.

I had this idea that if we could shine Bacon's knowledge like light through a prism we would splay a myriad of unending disciplines, a rainbow of knowledge. No doubt each discipline would have its own Ph.Ds. and each of them would admit to not having full knowledge of everything within their own domain. All of this change is daunting to the average man on the street. There is an overwhelming amount of information with details of any part of this vast spectrum known only to a very select few.

Much of the technology we deal with on a daily basis is beyond common understanding. It has been complexified and mystified. At the same time it operates beautifully and gives us a high degree of safety. Commercial airlines operate at a remarkably high safety rate and the planes can almost fly themselves. Medicine and dentistry are miraculous compared to the 1930s. Smart phones and their applications can manage many of our daily activities. Google gives us instant information. Most of this is wonderful but there is an aspect of unknowability which leads to complacency and unjustified reliance on performance and safety. And what is the most dangerous thing most Americans do every day? We all know the answer. It is driving our automobiles.

My first car was a 1951 Chevy Coupe that I purchased in 1960 for $165. If you popped the hood you would see an engine block mounted by a carburetor, an air cleaner, a dipstick and the ground beneath it all. The car was made out of metal. The interior was also metal. It had bench seats, no seatbelts, no airbags and no safety features. It had a speedometer and odometer, an ashtray, cigarette lighter, a radio and a clock that didn't work. The gearshift was on the steering column and the wind wings were the air conditioning. The tires were suspect, the brakes were marginal and the steering was mechanical. *But it did have plenty of power*! Highways were narrow and undivided and the death rate was more than four times what it is today. Saint Christopher medals were in high demand. If you are old enough and think back, you will realize that you knew someone who was killed or maimed in an automobile accident.

Today's cars are remarkably safe. In an accident they crush, absorbing the energy that used to be passed along to the passengers. Seat and shoulder belts are required. There are head restraints for whiplash. The car is operated by computers and the dashboard tells you everything you need to know but your pulse rate. If you were perchance to open the hood, you would not be able to tell that there was an engine block inside.

Given all of this there is a complacency that goes with driving today that is truly dangerous. An easy proof of this is a generalized use of the smart phone, especially texting, while driving. This is the leading contender for the **KNUCKLEHEAD** award. You would never try to do this driving my '51 Chevy. But an even larger problem is the complacency that leads to drivers who have no understanding of the nature of the beast beneath them.

As danger retreats and technology becomes more complicated, are we to give up diligence for ignorance and mythology? Have we done the Reverse Bacon? Living in such complexity have we relegated ourselves to total ignorance? No doubt we will never understand all of the theory, the nuances and the detail, but that doesn't excuse us from learning the basic facts that enable us to protect ourselves when driving. Have we gone from the One Man who knew everything to the Everyman who knows nothing?

* * *

"N" IS FOR KNUCKLEHEADS

Recent scandals at Toyota and General Motors are instructive with respect to driving safely.

First let's discuss the Toyota debacle. You will recall that Toyota was reported to have sold automobiles that had accelerators that would stick, causing the car to speed out of control. This was widely reported over quite a long period of time. The reason for the acceleration seems to have been determined to be the carpet on the driver side holding the gas pedal down. Whatever the reason, it is clear that if Toyota was selling cars that had accelerators that would stick, was selling cars with a defect that could potentially cause serious injury or death, it should be held responsible.

I was struck by the fact that in all the reportage of this potential disaster no one ever bothered to point out that there are easy steps that can be taken by the driver to greatly reduce the possibility of harm.

As you should know, if the accelerator sticks, simply moving the gear shift from drive ("D") to neutral ("N") disengages the engine from the drive wheels. If you don't know what "N" means, you definitely qualify for the **KNUCKLEHEAD** award. In neutral, your car will continue to coast down the road. You will still have power steering, power brakes and your airbag will work. At that point you put on your right turn signal, pull over to the edge of the road and put on the brakes. Your car will stop and then you can turn off the engine, pick up your cell phone and call a tow truck.

Alternatively, if you don't want to put your car in neutral for some unexplainable reason, you can simply turn off the ignition. This will stop the engine from running and accordingly stop the acceleration, but you will lose power steering, power brakes and your airbag. You will continue to have steering and brakes, although they will be stiffer (just like the old days), but you can steer your car to the curb, stop it and call the tow truck.

It seems to me that responsible media, when covering the Toyota acceleration problem, should spend seconds reminding people what to do in the event that were to happen to them. I have yet to hear anyone in the media mention how to solve the problem. This seems very peculiar. After all, this is life and death. Are we to believe that the people in the media don't know what the "N" on the gear shift is for? And frankly, the way they announce it, it sounds as though death is certain. Your car will simply continue to accelerate until you hit 150 mph and crash and die. It just seems irresponsible that they don't call attention to either the gearshift or the ignition switch.

Now to the General Motors' problem. Not long ago, General Motors underwent a corporate disaster concerning the fact that some of its automobiles were sold with an ignition switch that would, under certain circumstances, shut off the engine causing the risk of injury or death to increase. This defect has been implicated in a number of deaths. The question I want to discuss here has nothing to do with the responsibility of General Motors for any of the injuries or deaths that were caused by this defective switch. Just like Toyota, this is a life-and-death situation and it is ongoing.

As reported, the problem occurs when the driver has hung a variety of heavy items on his keychain so that as the car goes down the highway the key can be pulled from the "on" position to an "off" position. The engine stops and the car has then lost its power steering, power brakes and its airbag. The way this is reported implies that you have lost all your steering and your brakes. The media is silent about the fact that you still have steering and brakes although they are stiffer than they would be with power.

The actual situation the driver is left in is an automobile which continues to roll down the highway with reduced steering and braking but with the ability to pull the car over to the shoulder and stop. It is also important to remember that, given the nature of the defect, it's likely that if the driver shifts to neutral and turns the key to "on" the engine will start again.

To emphasize, I am ***not*** saying that the defect may not put the driver in some very dangerous situation which causes harm and or death for which GM is responsible. What I ***am*** saying is that if it occurs the car can remain under control, although it is lessened due to lack of power steering and brakes. In fact, this defect is *less dangerous* than running out of gas. If you run out of gas you have the same problem. The engine stops but you can't restart it as you probably can with respect to this defective switch.

Is there no obligation on a responsible media to point out the obvious potential solutions to a dangerous problem? Turn on the engine again and steer to the shoulder!

VERITIES, VACCINES AND VERISIMILITUDES[4]

In the same vein as the highly safe computer-driven automobile, we have modern medicine which is nothing short of miraculous in its efficacy, but just as opaque in its ability to be understood. Almost all of us are health-conscious and we are given a daily diet of ideas and suggestions for how we can lead a more healthy life. Do not smoke, do exercise, eat fruits and vegetables, cut down on red meats, and on and on and on. Sometimes what we hear on Monday is contradicted by what we hear on Friday. Nevertheless, we continue to listen and adapt and hope for the best. Even though it may be difficult to understand, we do tend to listen to our physician's advice and do our best to follow it. This is of course with one giant exception: vaccinations.

Which brings us back to Bacon. According to Barzun, for Bacon, "The notion that something is true because a wise man said it is a bad principle. Is the thing true in fact, tested by observation?" The new tool consists of applying this test. Observe closely, record findings exactly, and frame generalities that cover the facts, without coloring from myth, poetry, or other preconceived idea. "Go to the earth and it shall teach thee."[5] The rough translation today goes like this: You are entitled to your own opinions, but not to your own facts.

A verity, according to the Oxford English Dictionary (OED), is the truth—the true or real facts or circumstances. The verities of the vaccination are well-known, well understood and appalling.

Smallpox has been with us since 10,000 B.C. It was fatal to more than half of the people who contracted it. The vaccine (cow pox) was developed by Edward Jenner in 1796. Due to these vaccinations it was eradicated from the face of the earth before the end of the 20th century. Nevertheless, in the 20th century it is believed to have caused between *300 and 500 million deaths.*

In 1885 Louis Pasteur developed the vaccine for rabies. In the 1930s antitoxins and vaccines were developed for diphtheria, tetanus, anthrax, cholera, plague, typhoid and tuberculosis. In the 1950s vaccines were developed for polio, mumps, rubella and measles. Presently we also have vaccinations for influenza. In 1918 the Spanish flu killed roughly 50,000,000 worldwide and 675,000 in the United States.

Now for some personal observations. Those who presently refuse to get vaccinations have the luxury of knowing that there is a reduced likelihood that their children will be infected because others have been willing to get vaccinations. Were it otherwise, the diseases would still be rampant and there would be no arguments because fear would take over.

My mother, my grandmother and my aunt all contracted the Spanish flu and survived. At the same time my father was a soldier stationed at Camp Fremont near Palo Alto, and he said there were caskets in stacks for soldiers dying of the flu. My mother also survived typhoid.

As youngsters we all received smallpox vaccinations. There was no option. A scar was left from the vaccination and we all had a good time comparing scars. Personally I had chickenpox, a couple of different kinds of measles, mumps, whooping cough, and together with all my friends we spent most of our growing-up years terrified of getting polio. In my fifth-grade class were twin boys. One contracted polio and died overnight while the other twin did not contract it at all. Many of our family friends contracted it and were left with lifelong disabilities and others died. Rubella was about and if you contracted it during the early stages of pregnancy you stood a very high risk of having a baby with a serious birth defect. This happened to more than one of our friends. In 1957 when I was a sophomore in college and the bird flu hit, 70,000 people died in America in a matter of a couple of months. If that were to happen again I think the number of refusals would drop to zero.

But we do have many refusals. They are based in part upon the low risk that they will actually contract the disease because other people have been vaccinated. Refusals are also frequently based on something heard on television or read in the newspaper which has no basis in fact—the Verity. They have heard that after a vaccination someone was diagnosed with autism or some other malady. *Post hoc ergo propter hoc*, or, "after that therefore because of that."

A more recent example is the outbreak of measles in California. Starting from an initial exposure in Disneyland (presumably from an infected foreign visitor), fifty cases developed in the west and then spread to 17 other states and the District of Columbia, with more than 120 cases reported, most among children whose parents had refused to vaccinate them.

The refusals subject them to risk of illness and even death. The same applies when made for their children who have no choice. And this recalls to my mind and suggests something very similar—the verisimilitude!

Members of the Jehovah's Witnesses believe that it is against the teachings of the Bible to receive a blood transfusion. Occasionally a member's child will be in need of a blood transfusion in order to survive and the parents will refuse to permit it. The media tends to pick up these stories and seem to be a bit surprised when courts require that the child receive the blood transfusion in spite of the parents' wishes. The courts recognize that the child is incapable of making that decision and prefers to have it reach majority and have an opportunity to decide then what it will believe.

In what respect is a vaccination different from the situation when the parent refuses to have a child receive a blood transfusion? The science is clear. Vaccinations work. The difference seems to be the attenuated nature of the harm. In one case the child will surely die; in the other, the child may never contract the disease. But it is also true that the risk of contracting the disease is much greater without the vaccination. It seems certain that if the child is bitten by a rabid animal and the parents refused treatment, the court would step in. Right? And what about tetanus or plague or polio? They are all still around—but rare.

At what point is it reasonable for a court to allow a child to go unvaccinated because of a parent's refusal? Shouldn't the court err on the side of the child? Who speaks for the child? Refusals are bringing back many diseases. If polio resurfaces no doubt refusals will drop. What does that say about parents taking risks with their children's health?

BACON: KNOWLEDGE IS POWER[6]

Not so fast. Been to Washington lately? There are many members of Congress, both House and Senate, who routinely declaim that they don't believe in science. They reject knowledge. But they still have a vote. To them, *belief trumps science!*

In 2012 several candidates to become President of the United States said they did not believe in evolution. When it comes to climate change the rejection of science is almost automatic among many members of Congress.

One of the most curious positions on climate change came from the Speaker of the House. He said that we exhale carbon dioxide and that he didn't believe it was carcinogenic. It is hard to know where to begin to respond to that. The rejection of the science of evolution seems to be *religion-based* while the rejection of the science of climate change seems to be *oil-based.*

According to Bacon, "There is no magic hat in science; everything taken from the hat in works must first be put into it by observation or experiment."[7] Belief has nothing to do with it. Steven Jay Gould, one of the great scientists of evolution, asks, "How can a war exist between two vital subjects with such different appropriate turfs—science as an enterprise dedicated to discovering and explaining the factual basis of the empirical world, and religion as an examination of ethics and values?"[8] Good question.

How do we deal with the fact that so many in Congress do a "Reverse Bacon" and reject science? Perhaps if the media would start treating Luddites as Luddites? Yes?

* * *

"Shouldn't there be only nine of us up here?"

Chapter 2

The Supreme Court:
The Ultimate Polity and Final Arbiter (Or, They Didn't Learn That in Law School)

INTRODUCTION

All things partisan are also political but not all things political are necessarily partisan. Many controversial Supreme Court decisions, which have been called activists, are actually political but not necessarily partisan. If one mentions the Supreme Court and a political decision in the same breath, the immediate responses will be to refer to <u>Bush v. Gore</u>, a case that stands alone as entirely partisan, having directly interfered with the electoral process. If any decision has impacted the Court's credibility in recent times, it was this decision. What follows in this Chapter is an analysis of certain political decisions of the Supreme Court, many of which I believe were correct given the times and circumstances when they were made. Even though they fell outside the scope of what the Court should be doing, many of them have been the right thing for the country and are not, in the final analysis, partisan.

NOT IN LAW SCHOOL

One of the Court's most controversial decisions of the post-World War II era is <u>Roe v. Wade</u>.[9] There isn't a law school in the country that teaches at what stage of a pregnancy medical termination should be considered criminal. And yet, in a decision supported by five Republican appointed justices and passing 7 to 2, the Court decided that it would be un-constitutional to imprison anyone for terminating a pregnancy within the first trimester. While I personally agree with the policy articulated by the Court, it's pretty tough to find that in the Constitution.

How did this come about? Well, the year was 1973. The summer of love in San Francisco was only five years old. Free love was about and the pill had only been around for a few years. Women of all classes and financial circumstances were dealing with pregnancies. Abortions were illegal across most of the 50 states and were highly risky, often resulting in medical problems, including death. Given various religious and cultural beliefs, the chance that Congress or any state legislature would act was nil. Enter now our ultimate polity, the Supreme Court, to solve the problem when all else fails.

Think of it this way. It's frequently easier to accept bad news when you take it for what it is. Perhaps you've had an experience like this: you've had a very bad cold for a long while and haven't been able to shake it. You finally decide to go to the doctor. She tells you that you have a fairly serious case of pneumonia. Your first reaction is worry, upset and maybe even a little anger, but as you reflect on it you think "Well, now at least I know what it is and now I will be able to deal with it."

That is the way you should think about these particularly divisive Supreme Court decisions. Once you accept them for what they are it's much easier to deal with them. They are political, so get over it.

Another great example is Brown v. Board of Education.[10] It was decided in 1954 and held that the Equal Protection Clause of the 14th Amendment prohibited racial segregation in schools. The Court states that separate schools were inherently unequal. But we all know that various things that are separate can certainly be equal—anything from the DNA of identical twins to the goalposts at either end of a football field. Many things that are separate can be equal. The real holding of the case was that racial segregation in education is illegal in America.

In 1954 Jim Crow was alive and well across the South. Unless you lived through that era it's hard to describe how bad it was and how furious people were at the Supreme Court's unanimous decision in Brown v. Board of Education. The 14th Amendment's Equal Protection Clause certainly doesn't indicate that it was intended to deal with education as opposed to the more obvious things like voting rights and civil rights, but it was a problem that wasn't going to get solved without the Court's intervention.

President Eisenhower had to send federal troops into Little Rock, Arkansas, to integrate the schools there. If you haven't seen the film of that near-riot, it is definitely worth viewing. While racial discrimination was present across America, it was deeply embedded in the South. The Brown decision was one of the major factors in the Civil Rights Movement; in fact it was the spark that launched the movement. It was a great decision but no doubt a political one. The case reversed the holding of Plessy v. Ferguson[11] decided in 1896. The law had not changed in the intervening years. What had changed *were the views of the Justices* about race. What had not changed, and what was not going to change without the decision in Brown, was the overt racism in the South.

Other easy examples of matters decided by the Supreme Court that are not taught in our law schools include obscenity and the meaning of the 8th Amendment's "Cruel and Unusual

Punishment" clause. Law schools can teach what has been decided in the past but what is obscene is in the mind of the jurist. As put by Justice Potter Stewart, "I know it (obscenity) when I see it." And when Justice John Paul Stevens joined the Court he believed that cruel and unusual punishment did not preclude capital punishment. But by the time he left the Court he thought it did. The law hadn't changed; the only thing that changed was his mind.

Any real doubt about the political nature of some of the Supreme Court's decisions should have been erased decades ago at the time FDR attempted to pack the Court. His ire was raised by the fact that the Supreme Court continuously found New Deal legislation to be unconstitutional. One of the Court's decisions, in early 1936, was particularly problematic, holding state minimum wage laws unconstitutional. FDR announced his court-packing plan (to expand the Court to up to 15 members) in February, 1937. Not as well-known is the fact that Herbert Hoover and the Congress of the United States had at the same time been working to limit the power of the Supreme Court. In any event, *one month* after FDR announced his court-packing plan, the Supreme Court did a 180-degree reversal from the case it had decided just one year earlier and found that state minimum wage laws were now constitutional! FDR lost the battle—the number of justices remained at nine—but won the war. Thereafter, the Supreme Court routinely held New Deal legislation to be constitutional. The Supreme Court's reversal became known as "The switch in time that saved nine."[12]

Another very important case that demonstrates the point is Wesberry v. Sanders.[13] Decided in 1964, it found that all congressional districts should have roughly the same population base—one person/one vote—so that everyone in America voting for their Congress member would have equal voting rights. The decision was based upon the wording of Article 1, Section 2, of the Constitution, which as stated by the Court: "provides that Representatives shall be chosen 'by the People of the several States' and shall be 'apportioned among the several States....according to their respective numbers.' "

In reaching its conclusion, the Court relied on its reading of various arguments made at the Constitutional Convention. Weighing against this analysis: first, the language quoted doesn't bear the meaning ascribed to it and, had the Convention meant it, it could have said so clearly; second, for over 160 years congressional districts had unequal populations; third, the whole notion of equality didn't appear in the Constitution until the 14th Amendment was enacted in 1868; and finally, the Court's decision was handed down in February, 1964, in the midst of a great civil rights upheaval and just months before the enactment of the Civil Rights Act.

Not to make too fine a point of it, but civil rights and equality were in the air so much so that just four months later the Court decided <u>Reynolds v. Sims</u>,[14] which used the 14th Amendment's Due Process Clause to require all state legislatures to be one person/one vote.

In 1964 the southern states of America were under siege, and Congress was also under siege as the American public was appalled by what was happening in the South. The Supreme Court was doing its best to get equality in voting for everyone. Litigation to support the Voting Rights Act was underway in the South and it would take another year before the Voting Rights Act would be passed. <u>Wesberry v. Sanders</u> and <u>Reynolds v. Sims</u> were necessary products of political inequality and were decided by the Supreme Court with the knowledge that neither Congress nor any of the state legislatures would ever be able to make the necessary changes to get it done.

SUBSTANTIVE DUE PROCESS

Before the enactment of the 14th Amendment only the Federal Government was bound by the provisions of the Bill of Rights. In theory a state could limit free speech or freedom of the press, establish a religion, and take your property without paying for it. Then came the 14th Amendment requiring that states could not "deprive any person of life, liberty, or property without due process of law." What did this mean? Process is process and substance is substance. They are typically seen as antithetical concepts. Could the state limit free speech so long as it gave you "due process"? Well, it took the Supreme Court to decide that, as far as it was concerned, process and substance were the very same thing. Process meant substance. Accordingly, the Due Process Clause of the 14th Amendment has incorporated *against* the states many of the substantive provisions of the Bill of Rights.[15]

This has become known as *substantive due process* and correctly has been called an oxymoronic phrase. Many learned writers have attempted to explain how the substance of a law can be included within the phrase "due process of law." Their arguments are pure sophistry, generated to advance the notion that the Supreme Court's rulings in this regard have not been blatantly political. I suppose I should note here that I happen to agree with what the Supreme Court did; I just don't believe the actions taken can be hidden under a pretense that they were in any way derived from a fair reading of the Constitution.

The 13th, 14th and 15th amendments to the Constitution were enacted to provide for the end of slavery, to protect former slaves, and to provide other measures deemed necessary in the wake of the abolition of slavery. In order to protect those being freed, the 14th Amendment demanded that they be provided with due process of law and equal protection of the law. There is no indication that this was meant to incorporate *against* the states any of the provisions of the Bill of Rights. In fact, what one might anticipate was that due process of law was meant to supplant *lynchings*.

The Supreme Court's adoption of Substantive Due Process, whatever its origins, has had great and beneficial effects on American politics and culture. As America grew, various states had inconsistent and sometimes unconscionable laws that needed to be made consistent with or found to be illegal under the Constitution. I believe the Supreme Court saw that it was its role to bring this about and to create a consistent legal system throughout the country to protect the civil rights of all of its citizens. Accordingly, through the magic of Substantive Due Process, all states must provide: Free speech, <u>Gitlow v. New York</u> (1925); free exercise of religion, <u>Cantwell v. Connecticut</u> (1940); free press, <u>Near v. Minnesota</u> (1931); no cruel and unusual punishment, <u>Robinson v. California</u> (1962); no double jeopardy, <u>Benton v. Maryland</u> (1968); right to counsel in criminal cases, <u>Gideon v. Wainwright</u> (1963); no self-incrimination, <u>Malloy v. Hogan</u> (1964) and so on and so forth.

Without the Supreme Court's political interventions, America would still be completely balkanized. With what the Court has accomplished, we are a more unified nation. And that is good.

CONSERVATIVES AND LIBERALS

Politics is a dirty word these days. But remember, there are only two kinds of people in this world, whether it's within the company you work for or as citizens of the United States of America: there are those who like things the way they are, (retaining power and/or wealth) and there are those who would like to change things (redistributing power and/or wealth). The first are conservatives and the latter are liberals. Liberals like change; most people hate change, therefore most people hate liberals. If you were to listen to the way Republicans categorize Democrats and apply it to the Sun King, Louis XIV, you would have to say that he was a liberal! Yes? After all, according to Republicans all the Democrats want is a big strong central government with high taxes and lots of bureaucrats. That sounds a lot like Louis XIV to me. Actually, being a liberal or a conservative simply depends on your attitude. If you are in a capitalist country a liberal would be a socialist. On the other hand, if you are in a communist country a liberal would be a capitalist. That's why all the conservative pundits love liberals in China but hate them in America.

Getting back then to our Supreme Court. When the liberals are in charge we get change, and when the conservatives are in charge we get rulings that promote the status quo. If you are a person who wants to keep things as they are you are probably doing pretty well. You either have wealth or power or perhaps both. Nothing wrong with that. If you want to elect someone to help you preserve that position you will probably want to use your wealth and your power to get that accomplished. Nothing wrong with that either—so long as it's legal. The Supreme Court of today has gone a long way towards helping you achieve your goal. In <u>Citizens United</u>,[16] the Court made unlimited spending to support your candidate legal in many important ways. This of course allows liberals to do the same, but those who have wealth and power and want to preserve it typically will have more wealth and power to use than those who are trying to change the system. So we see a case of <u>Citizens United</u> as an effort by the Supreme Court to help maintain the status quo. And that is all right, that's what the conservatives are there to do.

CONSTITUTIONALLY PROTECTED CORRUPTION

However, having cast the die, the Court was then challenged to define the corruption that typically goes with spending vast amounts of money on political campaigns. Accordingly, in <u>McCutcheon v. FEC</u>[17] the Court articulated what kind of corruption is permissible under the Constitution and what is not.

Chief Justice Roberts wrote:

"Congress may target only *a specific type of corruption*—quid pro quo corruption…. Spending large sums of money in connection with elections, but not in connection with an effort to control the exercise of an officeholder's official duties, does not give rise to quid pro quo corruption. Nor does the possibility that an individual who spends large sums may garner 'influence over or access to' elected officials or political parties."

Thus, *the only type of corruption* that can be constitutionally made illegal is quid pro quo corruption. That leaves other kinds of corruption, occasioned by spending vast sums to get influence and access, *constitutionally prohibited* from being illegal. Strange.

Is it not entirely possible that circumstantial evidence could show that an individual who spends large sums of money to acquire influence or access to an elected official has managed to get to the point of being "quid pro quo" corrupt? Certainly you can be convicted of many crimes without any direct evidence. I assume it would be no different for proving that "legal corruption" actually turned into quid pro quo corruption. Correct?

And speaking of corruption, try this one on for size: After the school shooting in Newtown, poll after poll across America showed that 85 to 90% of the population favored better background checks before allowing someone to purchase a gun. It was defeated in Congress. In America the "democracy" there is no plausible answer for this except to say Congress is corrupt. Congress *is* corrupt. Would the Supreme Court find this to be the noncriminal type of corruption? Talk about an oxymoron.

One last observation concerning these high-level controversial decisions. Only a **KNUCKLEHEAD** would miss the fact that it is presently possible with near certainty to predict the vote of eight of the Justices of the Supreme Court. In these cases, each Justice gets the same brief, has the same facts, and they all have brilliant law clerks. And yet with each of these "activist" decisions it is certain how eight of them will vote. None of their votes are based on what they learned in law school, although they may be based upon what they learned in grammar school or at the knee of their Sunday school teacher. No one could miss the fact that the decisions are political. In every presidential election one of the reasons given for a person's vote is the prospect of whom the winner of the presidency will appoint to the Court. I assume this would provide a clue to the nature of the beast.

On the other hand, it is the Supreme Court that has stepped into the breach frequently to do the right thing. Stated another way, our government really doesn't work very well, even in the best of times. Given the gerrymander in the House and the crazy rules that run the Senate and the complicated system set up by the Constitution, it's hard even in the best of times to get anything done in Washington. These days it's almost impossible. No doubt a strong argument can be mounted that our present government is broken. But at least we have the Supreme Court that can step into the breach and keep things moving either to the left or the right. At the very least we get a decision. Bad decisions may be corrected; no decisions are the death of any organization or country.

THE IMPERIAL COURT

There are three things going on with the Court that in the long term could spell big trouble for it. First, the Court has been all too ready to find laws passed by Congress and signed by the President to be unconstitutional. Recently it found one of the provisions of the Voting Rights Act to be unconstitutional. It had passed the Senate 98 to 0 and the House 390 to 33. And yet by a vote of 5 to 4, the Court found one of its provisions unconstitutional.

It takes a two-thirds vote by Congress just to *initiate* a Constitutional Amendment, and yet the Supreme Court by a simple majority can overrule a federal statute on constitutional grounds. The Supreme Court established its right to do so in the landmark decision of <u>Marbury v. Madison</u>.[18] Few now argue with that decision but at the same time <u>Marbury</u> didn't say by *what vote* it could do so. Perhaps, on an equal dignity's argument, Congress could require six votes on the Court to overrule a federal statute. Makes sense to me. Two-thirds for Congress, two-thirds for the Court.

The second problem at the Court is that of recusal. Presently it is up to the individual justice to decide whether or not to be recused from any given case. Most courts have rules and procedures that allow litigants to raise the question of recusal. The Supreme Court does not. If the Court intends to retain its reputation for impartiality it should put forth procedures to allow litigants to raise questions of recusal just as it would be true in any other court.

Finally, as I mentioned at the beginning of this Chapter, there is the decision in <u>Bush v. Gore</u>, where the Court elected a president who had not won the popular vote. Three of the justices voted for Bush while four voted for Gore. Two justices did not record their vote. The Court's decision was an unsigned "per curiam" (by the Court) decision. Obviously the Court survived the controversy that its decision caused but the past is not always a good predictor of the future. In line with that thought, there has been much commentary in the press that the Chief Justice's vote to find the Affordable Care Act constitutional was motivated in part to protect the reputation of the Court. Enough said. There must be a limit to just how political the Court can get. For a more in-depth analysis of <u>Bush v. Gore</u> see Chapter 8.

©Charles Addams. Used with permission.

Chapter 3

The Truth About Lying

GEORGE WASHINGTON AND THE CHERRY TREE (THE BACK STORY)

Augustine Washington was a Virginia plantation owner. He grew tobacco and owned many slaves. Among his children was George Washington, our first president. As a youth George struck up a friendship with another youngster, a slave named Tom, who was just a bit older than George. Other than tobacco, Augustine had a few fruit trees for the family. It was autumn and the trees were bare and many of them were past their prime—all except one cherry tree. Augustine told his slave master, Simon, to have one of the slaves cut down all the old fruit trees but to save the cherry tree. Simon called Tom over and told him of his instructions from Augustine and directed him to take care of chopping down the fruit trees. George was nearby and heard both conversations. Tom, just a youngster, and with the trees being bare, couldn't tell one from another. He mistakenly cut down the cherry tree. George, who had gone into the plantation home briefly, returned and saw what had happened. He also saw Simon heading over and knew that when he realized what had occurred he was going to give Tom a real beating. Just then Augustine also saw what had happened and was heading in the same direction.

When they all arrived George stepped forward and said to his father, "I cannot tell a lie. I cut down the cherry tree." Tom said nothing. Augustine was angry, but told George, "Given your honesty, I will not punish you."

As George and his father walked back to the plantation house George turned to him and said, "I want to tell you the whole story." He then related exactly what had happened. Augustine was furious. He said, "You have interfered with Simon's control over the slave Tom who should have been punished for what he did." He then gave George a bit of a thrashing for having interfered with Simon's work and also for having lied about cutting down the cherry tree. The end.

Your assignment? Write a 250-word essay setting forth the relative moral positions of each of the actors in the story. Just kidding.

THE "L" BOMB

In certain contexts the word "liar" is one of those "bomb" words just like the "N" bomb or the "F" bomb. It can be, in certain contexts, the "L" bomb. I have been a civil trial lawyer for more than four decades and have noticed that trial lawyers rarely use the "L" bomb when addressing a judge or a jury unless it is towards the end of the case and they are firmly convinced that the judge and the jury have already come to the conclusion that the witness is in fact a liar.

This is also true in the public square. Politicians, too, stay away from the "L" bomb. Lawyers and politicians have a string of euphemisms for it. In ascending order, one finds: Factual inaccuracies, untruths, falsehoods, fabrications, prevarications and last, and only used by those who have attended some fancy east coast school, mendacious.

On the other hand, there is a recurring study reported every few years in the media by one group or another that *we all LIE roughly ten times a day.* How do we put that together with the dreaded "L" bomb? The answer requires us to define what we really mean when we say someone is lying.

THE BIBLE SAYS
The King James Version of the Bible gives us one of the Ten Commandments as: "Thou shall not bear false witness against thy neighbor." That sounds pretty heavy. My guess is that among those ten lies we supposedly tell every day, the study would include the following: your good friend Fred walks up wearing his new sport coat which he obviously thinks looks great. He asks, "Look at my new sport coat. What do you think?" You think it looks like something he got at a garage sale. He is, however, your good friend and you see no reason to insult him. You say, out of the goodness of your heart, "Fred, I think it looks terrific." In what possible sense is this "bearing false witness against your neighbor?" It's not *against* him, it's *for* him. In fact, it is the right and moral thing to do. It should never be thought of as a lie.

A lesser included thought in all of this might be: Of what value is your taste in sport coats anyway? I was taught in high school the old Latin maxim: *de gustibus non est disputandum*—in taste there is no argument. A good rule to follow.

In fact, the whole idea of characterizing a misstatement of your present state of mind needs examining. Take Fred's sport coat, for example. Several days later, having seen him in the coat a few times, you may actually change your mind. Many thoughts come and go in our minds on a rather involuntary basis anyway. Occasionally we will have very dark thoughts that startle even ourselves. We often change our minds about what we think and believe. Misrepresenting our own state of mind may be a bit tricky. It may be difficult to accurately characterize what our state of mind is from time to time. Just something to think (and rethink) about.

LYING

The word "lie" connotes immorality. The Oxford English Dictionary (OED) defines it as: "A false statement made with intent to deceive." So:

John was standing on the street corner when his friend Pete came running up yelling, "Which way did Fred go and where is my gun? When I catch him I'm going to kill him." John knows where the gun is and that Fred went south. He responds, "I have no idea where your gun is and Fred went north." Does that qualify as a lie per the OED? Yes. Is it immoral? No. Should it be called a lie? No.

It is said that lying, without more, is legal. But it is also true that the "without more" is not only what makes it illegal but also what makes it into a real lie. Lying, "without more," is probably what makes nine, or perhaps ten, of those ten lies we tell every day *the right thing to do*. Tell your friends you enjoyed the dinner when you didn't. Tell your neighbor that her new baby is very cute when in fact she looks like Winston Churchill, and so on.

Perhaps a better definition of lying would be: "A false statement made with intent to deceive the person lied to and for the benefit of the person doing the lying." "I did not have sex with that woman." "This car only has 20,000 miles on it." You get the idea. Another way of saying the same thing is that if "love one another" is the primary thought behind the false statement, it's likely it shouldn't be called a lie.

A different aspect of "lying" is when we are asked a question by someone who has no right to the answer. Your friend or business associate asks you about your health or financial condition. They have no right to this information, they're just being nosy. "It is none of your business" doesn't work because they will assume the worst and repeat it that way. There is nothing immoral about responding, "Everything is just fine" whether or not you are sick and broke. Agree? I think so. No lie here.

A pretext is a particularly insidious lie. It is a two-part lie. The first is the pretext which is usually true, weapons of mass destruction to the contrary notwithstanding. Accordingly, in order to uncover the lie you must first get through the truth.

"I don't want to sell you my house because your car is badly maintained and your kids are unruly and I love my house and I think you would not take care of it." But the real reason is that the buyer is Black or Asian or Hispanic. Or "I am sorry, Miss Jones, but Fred is going to get the promotion because you have come in late three times this month," when the real reason is that she has refused the bosses' advances. It's a coward's way of lying, quite immoral and quite hard to prove.

We need to come up with a new vocabulary for what we have been calling a lie. It is similar to the way we use the word "love." We say we love everything from donuts to grandma. The Greeks have four different words for love: *Eros* for romantic love; *Storge* for familial love; *Philia* for friendship; and *Agape* for selfless love or charity. We need to come up with a similar list so that we don't have the idea that every time we make a false statement it is a lie. And "white lie" certainly does not work. It is an oxymoron. If it's white, it's not a lie.

TRUTH (AND THE WHOLE TRUTH)

Truth, too, can be tricky. And "the whole truth" even trickier. In civil litigation in America today, parties, through their lawyers, are able to question other parties and witnesses under oath in what are known as depositions. They are a haven for half-truths. By way of example, suppose there was an accident at Main and Central in downtown Sacramento and the person who was accused of causing the accident has previously stated in writing that he was not there at the time of the accident: 6 P.M. on June 22.

In his deposition he is asked, "Where were you at 6 P.M. on June 22?"

His answer? "I don't know."

Immediately the questioner knows that the witness is playing games with him.

A new question then, "What were you doing at 6 P.M. on June 22?

Answer: "I was driving my car.
Question: "Where were you going?
Answer: "To San Francisco.
Question: "Where did you start your trip?
Answer: "Sacramento.
Question: "When did you start your trip?
Answer: "5:45 P.M., June 22.
Question: "When did you arrive in San Francisco?
Answer: "7:30 P.M.
Question: "So the answer to where were you at 6 P.M. on June 22 is, 'I was driving my car between Sacramento and San Francisco.' Is that correct?
Answer: "Yes." (If it was his car. No, if not)

In other words, his original answer was not a lie because he doesn't know exactly where he was at 6:00 P.M. But it was only a half-truth because he knew he was in his car driving to San Francisco at the time. He answered as he did because his lawyer told him to answer questions in the narrowest way possible. His half-truth answer made the deposition tedious, long and difficult. That is an everyday practice in present day civil depositions. The witnesses are in fact sworn to tell the truth and the whole truth. They only respond to the first part of the oath.

TRUTHS? HALF-TRUTH? OR LIES?

1.   There is the apology "I am sorry if I offended you." Translation: he is not sorry, you're just too sensitive. The "I am sorry" part is a lie. Correct? What happened to "I am a young cowboy, and I know I done wrong." (*Streets of Laredo*.)

2.   There is the subject of compromise. Famously George H. W. Bush promised "no new taxes" and then raised taxes. According to Edmund Burke (who is presently considered an arch-conservative): "All government, indeed, every human benefit and enjoyment, every virtue, and every prudent act is founded on compromise and barter."[19] But compromise has become a dirty word in politics these days. And those who engage in it are frequently called "liars." Seen through Burke's

eyes, that certainly is not the case.

3. There is the question presented when a person, who represents that he is fact-driven, that he relies on the facts, that he is a fact-based decision-maker, rejects empirical evidence because it contradicts his belief system. How can those two things be reconciled "honestly?" When candidates for president say they don't believe in evolution or global warming, at least one of them must be lying? Please.

Truth can be devastating, and withholding it may sometimes be the right thing to do. You learn some very bad news just before a celebration. If asked, it is okay to deny knowledge until the party is over. Right?

An unusual example of this occurred recently. A medical doctor, an obstetrician/gynecologist, was found to have been taking pictures of women during his examinations. As reported by the media he had been fired and prosecuted. The story goes on to say that the women were all making claims for damages because of what he had done. The question is: Why were the women told? Without knowledge they haven't been psychically injured. I am not speaking as a lawyer, but as a human being that thinks "why should we cause the hurt?" I assume the answer is there was no way to keep this information private.

THE OMISSION

On another topic, can public silences be an implicit lie? In 1988 Michael Dukakis was running against George H.W. Bush for President. The savings and loan scandal was at full throttle. It was costing the economy hundreds of billions of dollars. It was caused by Congress passing a law signed by President Reagan that simultaneously deregulated savings and loans and raised federal insurance for deposits from $10,000 to $100,000. A real genius of a move. The savings and loan industry, which had been highly regulated, was now set loose upon the country to cheat, steal and lie and let the taxpayers pay for it. Dukakis and Bush both knew that the Democrats and the Republicans were equally responsible for the mess. It was never mentioned in the campaign. How does this measure up on the "L" bomb scale?

An even worse example is the investigation of what occurred on 9/11. After an enormous amount of pressure brought on the administration by the widows of the dads who had died in the Twin Towers, a "Bipartisan Commission" was appointed to do the investigation.

The chemical equivalent of a bipartisan commission is like adding something acidic to something basic. What you get has been neutralized. It is a group of politicians dedicated to saving each other's reputations. If you want to know what happened and who is responsible, what needs to be done is to hire the most aggressive Democratic prosecutor in the country and hire the most aggressive Republican prosecutor in the country, give them both adequate funding and have them each write a report. Read both reports and make up your own mind.

As a result of the "Bipartisan Commission" report and in spite of all the warnings that were floating around before 9/11—including knowledge of mid-eastern men learning how to fly jumbo jets without having to learn to land them—no one in the government *lost one day's pay*. Is this "The Big Lie"??

CONCLUSION

The entire subject of lying seems to be a classic case of exalting form over substance. What are the moral implications of any particular false statement of fact? Is it hurtful? It may be, but on the other hand it may be totally benign or helpful or charitable. I think when I was learning about lying, "sin" swallowed up the discussion. I know it can be complicated, but it is certainly worth thinking about.

THE
HOLY BIBLE

CONTAINING THE

Old and New Testaments

TRANSLATED OUT OF
THE ORIGINAL TONGUES AND WITH THE FORMER
TRANSLATIONS DILIGENTLY COMPARED AND REVISED

THE TEXT CONFORMABLE TO THAT
OF THE EDITION OF 1611 COMMONLY
KNOWN AS THE AUTHORIZED OR

King James Version

THE WORLD PUBLISHING COMPANY
CLEVELAND AND NEW YORK

Chapter 4

The Bible Says?
(Or What is a Testament?)

INTRODUCTION

If you profess to be a Christian or if you are a person who spends time attacking Christianity, why are you constantly quoting from the Old Testament? Don't you get it? There is a New Testament and just so you know, the word Testament, in Bible talk, means "Covenant with God." There is a *New* Covenant.

So when you hear a Christian say, "Have you heard the good news of the gospel," they mean that things have changed. Out with the Old and in with the New.

THE OLD TESTAMENT

As an example of the difference, the Old Testament, King James version, provides:

"And if any mischief follow, then thou shalt give life for life,

Eye for eye, tooth for tooth, hand for hand, and foot for foot,

Burning for burning, wound for wound, stripe for stripe."

Exodus 21: 23-25

"And if a man cause a blemish in his neighbor; as he hath done, so shall it be done to him:

Breach for breach, eye for eye, tooth for tooth: as he hath caused a blemish in a man, so shall it be done to him again."

Leviticus 24: 19-21

"And those which remain shall hear, and fear, and shall henceforth commit no more any such evil among you.

And thine eye shall not pity; but life shall go for life, eye for eye, tooth for tooth, hand for hand, and foot for foot."

Deuteronomy 19: 20-21

THE NEW TESTAMENT

On the other hand, the New Testament says to the contrary:

"Ye have heard that it hath been said, an eye for an eye, and a tooth for a tooth: but I say unto you, that ye resist not evil: but whosoever shall smite thee on thy right cheek, turn to him the other also.

"And if any man will sue thee at the law, and take away thy coat, let him have thy cloak also.

And whosoever shall compel thee to go a mile, go with him twain.

"Give to them that askest thee, and from him that would borrow of thee, turn not thou away.

"Ye have heard that it hath been said, thou shalt love thy neighbor, and hate thine enemy.

"But I say unto you, love your enemies, bless them that curse you, do good to them that hate you, and pray for them which despitefully use you, and persecute you; that ye may be the children of your father which is in heaven: for he maketh his sun to rise on the evil and on the good, and sends rain on the just and on the unjust."

The Gospel of St. Matthew 5:38-45

DISCUSSION

It is not possible to make consistent the above quoted verses from the Old Testament with those from the New Testament. They are antithetical. It should not come as any surprise that there are substantial differences between the Old and New Testaments. Their names rather give it away, don't they? Yes. So if you are an evangelical or a critic or a politician who either professes or criticizes Christianity you should have some basic understanding of what Jesus said and what he didn't say. For example, a politician who routinely professes his or her Christianity should not support capital punishment by calling on an "eye for an eye or a life for a life" from the Old Testament. Jesus didn't say that. He said "turn the other cheek."

So stop with all the Old Testament bugaboos. Jesus never mentions homosexuality or stoning anyone. In fact, one of the favorite Bible stories is the woman who had committed adultery and was about to be stoned. Jesus saved and forgave her saying, "Let the one of you without sin cast the first stone." I'm sure you remember that—so stop with the Old Testament stories. He didn't say anything about how long it took God to create the earth or how big Noah's Ark was supposed to be or whether Lot's wife really turned into a pillar of salt. Rather he gave us the Eight Beatitudes. Personally I've always liked: "Blessed are the peacemakers for they shall be called the children of God." We don't hear enough of that one these days.

Remember, Jesus spoke as a Jew. The Last Supper was a Passover Seder. He didn't reinvigorate the Ten Commandments. When asked to name the greatest commandment, he did not refer to them, but rather said it was, "First; love God, and second, love your neighbor as you love yourself." So if you profess to being a Christian you should give up on those Old Testament references and stick with the good news, you know, the lilies of the field, the Prodigal Son, the good Samaritan, forgiveness, feed the hungry, and visit the sick. Finally, we definitely should try to remember how to get that old camel through the eye of the needle![20]

CONCLUSION

Whether you are a bible thumping Christian or an out-spoken critic of Christianity, one thing is certain. In either case, you cannot use references from the Old Testament as part of your argument. Sorry, and Amen.

* * *

"Still, did you ever stop to think where you and I would be if it weren't for evil?"

Chapter 5

Sin or Jail:
(A Dichotomy of Gender)

The mere mention of the Catholic Church these days brings to mind the great scandal that has enveloped it in the last couple of decades. As I began to write this piece about the scandal, it prompted a memory of a story I used to tell young lawyers to see how adept they were at assessing responsibility. Here is the story:

A doctor and his family decided to take an extended vacation. They hadn't had one in a very long time and before they left the doctor took certain precautions. First he had an alarm installed on his home. Then he talked to his neighbor friend across the street and asked him if he would keep an eye on his house while they were gone. His neighbor said that he would. He then called the newspaper that he subscribed to and told it to stop the daily delivery. He also asked the gardener to be sure to take care of his home so it would not look like no one was there.

When the family returned from their vacation they found a pile of newspapers on the front porch and when they walked in the front door they found that they had been cleaned out. Televisions, all the electronic equipment, jewelry, all were gone. They checked and found that the alarm didn't work and on investigation learned that the gardener hadn't done anything until the day before they returned. When they turned to the neighbor across the street he admitted that he didn't believe anything would go wrong and he left on vacation about a day after the doctor had left. End of story.

The young lawyers were then asked to assess responsibility as among all of the players. Typically they found the neighbor and the alarm company most responsible. They were followed closely by the gardener and the paperboy. After giving them time for reflection I would then give them my answer which was, "It's the burglar!"

How does this apply to the Catholic Church scandal? Well, there are two parts of the scandal. First, there were many priests who were pedophiles abusing children. Second, there were even more priests who weren't pedophiles who allowed the "burglars" to get away with it for decades. How in the world did this happen?

My background? I went through 12 years of Catholic schools, eight years with the Holy Cross nuns and four years with the Christian Brothers. I was also an altar boy for many years, back when the Mass was celebrated in Latin. So when the scandal broke within the Church a couple of decades ago, I was totally shocked. No doubt pedophilia is as old as mankind itself. And there is no reason to think the clergy would be exempt. But I had no knowledge of any of these things. I didn't even know much about the whole subject of pedophilia let alone what was going on among priests. Shocked, I could not understand how this could have happened without the guilty priests—thousands of priests in dozens of countries—being turned over to the proper authorities. My own experience with the priesthood was that, just like other human beings, they had their frailties but they were men of goodwill and integrity, by and large. How could they have not seen what was happening and reported it?

In my days as an altar boy there was the great ritual of the Latin Mass that seemed to go on interminably. There was church music that actually sounded like church music, long lines for confession on Saturday night. I recall the smoky odor of candles burning, the smell of incense, sneaking tastes of communion wine. And finally, the mystery of the Catholic "sanctum sanctorum."

And above all the omnipresence of sin, it was everywhere, especially for a teenage boy—and its name was sex. As teenagers we used to joke that we could only find two things in the Ten Commandments about sex: adultery and coveting your neighbor's wife. We knew we weren't involved in adultery and coveting your neighbor's wife was out of the question since they were old ladies, as far as we were concerned. On the other hand, we could covet their daughters because that wasn't covered.

The pastor of our parish was a fiery fellow born and raised in Ireland who, from the pulpit during the WWII, referred to Churchill as a bloody cutthroat! He lost a few British parishioners over that one. The congregation included future Supreme Court Justice Kennedy and his family. One of my fellow altar boys was Jethro (Max Baer, Jr.). We were both terminated one Sunday after mass because during the service, when we were standing one step below the priest, we were both roughly six inches taller than he was. He thought we'd been there long enough.

At about the same time (1953) a movie was released entitled "I Confess." It starred Montgomery Clift and was directed by Alfred Hitchcock. Its storyline suggests one of the reasons why pedophile priests may have gotten by with it for so long.

In the beginning of the movie Montgomery Clift is a priest who hears a confession where the sin was murder. In a very unlikely turn of events Montgomery Clift's character is charged with the very same murder. This brings into sharp focus one of the problems that can be created by the "Seal of Confession." The priest, knowing who the murderer was, could not reveal it even though he was being charged with that very crime. Taken to its logical conclusion the priest could be convicted while maintaining the confidentiality of the confessional, allowing a murderer to go free and possibly murder again. This demonstrates the bitter fruit that can result by preferring privacy over guilt.

I saw the movie when it came out in 1953. Thinking back on it makes me wonder what the effect might be on a priest hearing confessions week after week, year after year, listening to all sorts of evils great and small.

Priests would hear everything from masturbation to mayhem. They would hear things that were criminal and things that were not. In fact it's good to recall that most things that are immoral are not criminal. When we define some actions as criminal, it isn't meant to regulate morality but to control civil order. And the Church is only interested in sin, not controlling civil order, so the distinction between what was simply immoral and what was actually criminal wasn't important in the confessional. They were both sinful and that was what was important.

Take the seven deadly sins, for example: pride, envy, gluttony, lust, anger, greed, and sloth. Without more they are all legal. Moreover most of the 10 Commandments are legal and all are sometimes legal. Lying, without more, is legal. Adultery in America is legal, although it might be a capital crime in some countries. Ignoring your parents in their old age in America is legal. Killing is frequently legal: justifiable homicide, war and executions. Even stealing is sometimes legal. Think of Hurricane Katrina and the woman taking food from the deserted grocery store to feed her children, versus someone smashing windows and walking off with a stereo in the New Orleans riots.

The point is that priests over some long period of time may become somewhat oblivious to the distinction between forgiving sins that are criminal and sins that are not criminal. In other words, the Church was about sin but not about criminality. Not only that, but the routine of confession became ritualistic, formulaic and automatic.

In the day of the Latin mass many young American boys were going into the priesthood as early as junior high school. After ordination they would be assigned to your parish with little or no knowledge of the world around them. They were sent to a life in the confessional hearing of wife beatings, child beatings, child molestations, drunkenness, fistfights, robbery and even perhaps murder. They would hear many matters having no chance of rising to the level of criminality, such as taking the Lord's name in vain, eating meat on Friday, missing Mass on Sunday and all kinds of sexual activity right down to having "impure thoughts." Each confession began with "Bless me Father for I have sinned" and ended with absolution— whether it was a peccadillo or a felony.

Obviously if Father Murphy were to come in and confess to being a pedophile, the priest hearing the confession would be unable to report it to anyone. But take the same priest who learns outside of the confessional what Father Murphy has been doing. Does he treat it as a felony or as a sin? Weighing heavily on his mind will be a desire to protect the Church—the Joe Paterno syndrome. Had it been learned in the confessional he would take Father Murphy's promise not to do it again as sufficient for absolution. Learned outside the confessional he slides into treating it as a sin rather than a felony and does not report it to the police, allowing Father Murphy to continue doing what he's done in the past. In the priest's mind, treating a crime as just a sin is rather routine. Moreover, the Catholic Church has no requirement that people who commit crimes be prosecuted. If you commit a murder it is a sin and that's the end of it as far as the Church is concerned. In other words, there is no doctrine, no Papal Bull or anything else in the Church that requires criminal penalties for sins that are criminal.

There are, of course, other potential reasons why the pedophiles weren't reported to the proper authorities. Ignorance and naïveté about pedophilia would likely be among them.

There is an element of child rape being so gross as to make it hard to really believe that it was going on, leading to the notion that it is all just rumor. And maybe there is a comparison to the policeman's thin blue line. Perhaps among the priesthood there's a thin white collar?

In any event, we have a long history of priests and bishops failing to report priests abusing children, thus allowing them to continue to abuse children.

Now for the denouement: Let us speak of abortion. After WWII, there was, across America, a growing demand for abortion even though it was criminal. Accordingly, women availed themselves of what came to be known as "back alley" abortions. Not only were they criminal but they were also very dangerous. Women were not only getting serious infections but also dying as a result of these illegal procedures. In order to help alleviate this problem, in 1967 California passed the Therapeutic Abortion Act. It was signed into law by Governor Ronald Reagan. The abortion rate in California quickly jumped from just over 500 to roughly 100,000 per year. This confirmed and emphasized the need for decriminalization.

Roughly six years later the Supreme Court in <u>Roe v. Wade</u> made history by decriminalizing certain abortions in America.[21] There was one clear ruling in the case: in America you will not go to jail for terminating a pregnancy within the first 12 weeks. The rest of the decision was a bit vague but basically held that after the first trimester your chances of going to jail increased with the length of the pregnancy. This is as one might expect.

What the Supreme Court did not decide was that abortions were a good idea, that they were moral, that you should have one, or that medically or psychologically it was a good thing to do. All it said was that under certain conditions you could not go to jail for having one.

Walter Cronkite was a wonderful man and a great influence for the good of American journalism. Like all of us he was not perfect and on one occasion he really put his foot in it. When <u>Roe v. Wade</u> was decided by the Supreme Court he went on television and in his most stentorian voice announced: "The

Supreme Court has legalized abortion." Wrong. What it did was to decriminalize some abortions. It did not legalize abortions any more than it legalized adultery or lying or ignoring your parents in their old age or your children when they were young. To say abortion was legalized implies that it is approved, and not just under certain conditions but in its entirety. Just think how the debate may have changed if he had said that the Supreme Court had decriminalized (rather than legalized) certain types of abortions. The Court made no judgment as to its morality. It only said that, like many other things of a questionable morality we all do during our lives, we won't go to jail for them.

The question is: How do we treat a woman who terminates a pregnancy at six weeks? Put her in jail or put our arms around her and give her support in what may well be a difficult time. You would think that a good Christian or a good Jew or a good Muslim or a good anything would choose the latter.

The Catholic Church in America has called for Roe v. Wade to be reversed. Implicit in this position is recriminalizing early-term abortions. This puts the Church in a very awkward position. It means that while it has not called the police on pedophiles, it is calling the police on women who have early term abortions. Clearly the Church believes they are immoral. But taking the position that women who have abortions should go to jail rather than to confession flies in the face of the Church's long-held position that criminal consequences of sin is left to the civil authorities.

Accordingly, we have pedophile priests not being reported to the authorities while at the same time women who have early-term abortions, according to the Church's position on Roe v Wade, would be reported to the police for jail time.

Based on my conversations with Catholic clergy I don't believe they have focused on the actual holding in Roe. Focusing as it does simply on jail time, I don't believe Roe v. Wade violates any doctrine of the Catholic Church. It seems to me that what would be best for the Church at this point is to concentrate on what Pope Francis is recommending, that its pastoral mission is helping the poor and needy.

* * *

"This toy is designed to hasten the! child's adjustment to the world around him. No matter how carefully he puts it together, it won't work."

Chapter 6

Guilty
(If Guilty)

We need to get something straight. If you are acquitted in a criminal trial in America it does not mean that you are innocent and it does not mean that *you're not guilty*. It means that the government wasn't able to persuade a jury that you were guilty beyond a reasonable doubt in order to make you live in a small cage, eat bad food and hang out with some pretty awful people.

You have heard that a defendant is innocent until proven guilty. That is not true. He is innocent if he is innocent and he is guilty if he is guilty. The legal process can't change that. The phrase you've heard so often simply means that the burden is on the government to prove that a person is guilty, which it may or may not be able to do. And it is a heavy burden. Accordingly, most criminals never go to trial. They are allowed to enter pleas to some lesser offense even though they are quite guilty. This happens for many different reasons: Overcrowded courts, questionably reliable witnesses and relevant evidence that has been suppressed by the court, just to name a few. Achieving justice can be very complicated. But guilty is guilty.

Lost in all the legal verbiage is the fact that we are each entitled to make up our own minds about the guilt or innocence of anyone charged with a crime. But you should be cautious about doing that unless you happen to be present at the trial so that you know all the facts that the jury knows, unless, of course, you are directly involved and have personal knowledge of the facts. In either case, and in spite of what you hear from the media, the defense attorney, or even the prosecutor, the most reliable facts are the circumstances surrounding the crime! Circumstantial evidence doesn't lie.

* * *

"The poor are getting poorer, but with the rich getting richer it all averages out in the long run."

Chapter 7

Civil Disobedience
(An Oxymoron?)

CIVIL CRIMES?

How does committing a crime become civil? Normally breaking the law is criminal. Correct? What then makes some criminality "Civil"? Even more to the point, how often have you heard of a criminal being referred to as "disobedient"? The last time I was referred to that way was when I got caught by one of the nuns in grammar school. By the time I turned fourteen I was called something a lot stronger than disobedient. Oh well.

Likely those involved in civil disobedience get this rather benign name because typically they are folks with some serious, probably moral, disagreement with a law they are trying to get changed. If they fail to effect change legally, they may decide to break the law and the key here is: They are willing to take responsibility for what they do and pay the consequences. Think of marchers in Selma, Alabama. They knew they would be arrested. It was a price they were willing to pay to call attention to something that was morally and legally wrong. Taking responsibility is why we have come to call it "civil" rather than "criminal." If you don't take responsibility for what you have done, you are just a crook. Yes?

A FAILED TEST

Not long ago a group of students was trespassing on the University of California, Davis, campus in a sit-in, protesting certain university policies. The police were there and had been ordered to remove the students. They repeatedly told them to move but they did not move. They repeatedly told the students that if they didn't move they were going to get pepper sprayed. They did not move—and they got pepper sprayed. At that point, had the students wiped their eyes and gone back to class, they would have passed the test. They would have taken the consequences and showed the stuff they were made of. But they did not. Rather, they complained loudly and then sued the university, thus flunking the test. Moreover, they accepted payment for settling their lawsuit, embarrassing themselves even further. There were no consequences for their actions. What was the point?

Great outrage ensued around the country as the video of the spraying went viral. I believe one of the policemen involved even suffered consequences to his career. Not seen on camera were the warnings that were repeated so often that the students had time to put on hats and pull up their hoods to protect themselves from the spray. Trial by video is not a good idea.

TRESPASSING AMERICAN STYLE

As distinguished from the great civil rights struggle in the south, I think civil disobedience as we now see it probably started in Berkeley in the fall of 1964 with the free speech movement. Sit-ins, Be-ins, Sleep-ins and trespassing of all kinds, shapes and sizes, to make a point about one thing or another, have become ubiquitous. Whether it is a mass invasion of the State Capitol building in Wisconsin or one strident environmentalist chained to a redwood tree, trespassing for a cause has become a regular part of the business of America. How or whether demonstrators reap their deserved consequences varies widely.

Blockading the Brooklyn Bridge will end swiftly with arrest. On the other hand, picketing a nuclear power facility without interfering with its operations might result in the demonstrators spending a lot of time without really being noticed. But in either event, implicit in each scenario would be the knowledge of the protesters that they were breaking the law by trespassing and their willingness to take the consequences if necessary.

VIETNAM WAR

The Vietnam War sparked all kinds of protests, but few of them would qualify as civil disobedience, starting with the most egregious, bombings and threats of bombings. On the other end of the spectrum would be many licensed protest parades around the country. In between it ran the gamut from a young man going to Canada to avoid the draft to the urban riot at the 1968 Chicago Democratic Convention. The point here is that none of those activists had any intention of ending up in jail. In summary, there were lots of laws broken and a great deal of civil unrest but not much that would qualify as civil disobedience.

WASHINGTON, D.C., LEAKS

There has been a strange marriage between the First Amendment and civil disobedience when it comes to the notorious practice in Washington of leaking information to the press. I say "notorious" rather than "famous" because the leaks almost always violate the law, and if not the law, they violate some condition of employment that could get you fired. The extraordinary aspect of this practice is that the leaks normally go to some rather well-known journalist who works for one of the major media outlets, usually a newspaper. The federal government takes the position that there is no shield law in effect protecting the journalist from disclosing sources. The question usually boils down to whether or not the prosecutor decides to proceed. Quite often there is no prosecution. It is often reported that there is a negotiation that goes on between the federal agency involved and the editorial staff of the newspaper that employs the journalist that has the information, with the end result that whether or not Mr. and Mrs. America learns of some leaked classified information will depend upon the decision of an unknown journalist.

As far as civil disobedience is concerned, neither the person who leaks the information nor the journalist who publishes it suffers any consequence for breaking the law. A curious arrangement.

EDWARD SNOWDEN

From all available information, it appears that Mr. Snowden went to work for the National Security Agency (NSA) with the specific intention of disclosing whatever information he found that offended his sensibilities. So far as has been reported it does not appear as though he made any effort to approach the agency with what it was he was about to disclose in an effort to get it rectified or ameliorated before he went ahead and produced it to the public. Moreover, it clearly appears that he was on his way to Hong Kong before the disclosure was made public. The most obvious aspect of what Mr. Snowden did was that *he never intended to take any responsibility* for his actions. If Snowden wanted to perform an act of civil disobedience in order to correct what he perceived to be a grievous wrong, he should have remained in the United States to tell his story. To run away and then to take refuge in Russia—that bastion of individual freedom, free press, and no surveillance of its citizens—was wrong.

On the other hand, the Congressional response to Snowden's disclosures has been less than inspiring. My impression of the response is that most of the members of Congress were generally *unaware* of the provisions of the law that they had passed. What the Foreign Intelligence Surveillance Act (FISA) permitted the federal government to do seemed to be news to them. The present law was enacted in 2008 to rectify and clarify many of the abuses of the prior Act by the Bush administration. And the previous FISA law had been enacted to curb similar abuses by the Nixon administration. You would expect Congress to have a better grasp of what it had done. The point of the Foreign Intelligence Surveillance Act is pretty well given away by its name. Aware of the fact that such surveillance may occasionally involve American citizens, provisions are made for that likelihood. In order to proceed in those circumstances a warrant is required from a federal judge, a so-called FISA judge. It's good to recall that a federal judge can, upon a showing of probable cause, issue a warrant allowing the federal government to wiretap our telephones and invade our homes, and search every inch of them, and be consistent with our Constitution. FISA judges are just like any other federal judge except for obvious reasons they must meet in secrecy. All of this is part of the law passed by Congress.

In summary, the law, while somewhat misguided, seems to be constitutional. The Congress that passed the law seems unaware of its provisions. The same Congress, since the disclosures, has amended it in a way that is cosmetic at best. And Mr. Snowden has proved himself to be a world-class **KNUCKLEHEAD.**

*"Do you ever have one of those days when every-
thing seems unconstitutional?"*

Chapter 8

Our Constitution: New and Improved

INTRODUCTION

Our present Constitution bears little resemblance to the Constitution as originally written by the Founding Fathers.[22] It has now been changed for the better by 27 amendments. They are, by definition, improvements, not stand-alone proclamations. They change the old to the new, effectively repealing everything that comes before that is inconsistent with them. Accordingly, the document which is the end result must be internally consistent. We should be able to draw a straight line through our original Constitution and all of its amendments and come up with one theory of government. Unfortunately, it is presently being interpreted in a way that makes it internally inconsistent. This has produced antithetical theories of government resulting in stalemate.

Change, as we all know, is the only constant. Institutions that cannot adapt to change do not survive. Our present Congress is unable to make major decisions for the country, yet we all know that decision-making is critical to survival.

THE ORIGINAL CONSTITUTION
It has been said that the Founding Fathers would be slack-jawed today at what has happened to the nation they created.[23] True enough. But what is also true is that we, too, would be slack-jawed today were the original Constitution suddenly to spring back to life. You will be shocked to learn that under the original Constitution you very likely had *no* vote.[24] You will find that you aren't the equivalent of Thomas Jefferson or George Washington but rather a member of the middle class or a woman (God forbid), or even worse, a black man and you have *no* vote. Even if it were to turn out that you are a white male property owner, you could only vote for your Congress*man*. Your Senators would be chosen by your state legislature and your President would be elected by men chosen as electors by the same state legislature.[25] And they could exercise their own judgment about their choice for President.[26]

You would also find that the Bill of Rights, which were demanded by the Anti-Federalists to restrict the power of the new federal government[27] did not apply to your state government. Accordingly, as Chief Justice Marshall held in Barron v. Baltimore, the state could take your property without just compensation.[28] Potentially then the state could try you twice for the same crime, conduct searches of your property without a warrant, establish a state religion and confiscate your guns. The states were truly sovereign at that time.

You would be living in a "Republic" specifically designed to "restrain the excesses of democracy."[29] In furtherance of that effort you would find that your resurrected Constitution guarantees to each state the right to be a Republic,[30] just like the one they originally created. No doubt a Republic can be designed to be democratic—where ours is now headed—but it was not so originally. It started as the very definition of an oligarchic Republic, a government controlled by the few. And under that Republic you will find no sign of the first principle of the Declaration of Independence: "All men are created equal." To the contrary, the only men created equal were white and at the top of the socio-economic ladder. Universal suffrage was rejected, slavery was legal and states, not people, were equal.

THE ROAD TOWARD DEMOCRACY

How did we get from that original Republic to a place where we have come to regard America as a democracy with one person/one vote? Well, there has been an inexorable movement in that direction and we have come a long way, but are not there yet. Like the Donner Party, those last few miles can be a killer.

By the time of the Civil War most white men had the right to vote for their Congressman. At its conclusion there were added three great amendments: The 13th abolished slavery while the 14th, *for the first time*, required the states to provide equal protection and due process to their citizens; the 15th extended the vote to all without regard to "race, color or previous condition of servitude."

The intent of these three amendments was immediately subverted by the Klan, Jim Crow laws, poll taxes, literacy tests and deep-seated racism. This went unchecked until World War II, at the earliest, when women in the workforce and blacks in the Armed Forces began a series of movements aimed at finding equality for all Americans. The move toward a democratic Republic had also been given a huge boost by the 17th Amendment which provided for a direct election to the Senate and the 19th, 24th and 26th Amendments, finally giving the vote to women, and then to the poor and young adults.

THE 14TH AMENDMENT

It was the 14th Amendment that saved the day and has ever since led the battle for equality. The story begins in 1954 with the Supreme Court's decision in <u>Brown v. Board of Education</u>[31]

holding that separate was no longer equal. School segregation was illegal and the National Guard was sent into Little Rock, Arkansas by President Eisenhower to enforce the law. Brown was the spark and the catalyst for the Civil Rights movement that continues today.

The importance of the 14th Amendment to our constitutional form of government cannot be exaggerated. For the first time in our history the states and the federal government were required to afford us equal protection and due process. It is important to know that the Federal Government is also bound by the same rules of equality and due process as those imposed on the states by the 14th Amendment. The Supreme Court's "approach to the 5th Amendment equal protection claims has always been precisely the same as to equal protection claims under the 14th Amendment."[32] As lawyers like to say, when the Supreme Court decided that education was covered by equal protection and that racially segregated schools were therefore illegal, "the floodgates were opened." It was truly a sea change. The original Constitution was *not* about equality, in fact, just the opposite, very restricted voting rights and slavery was legal.

THE DUE PROCESS CLAUSE AND THE 14th AMENDMENT

There is a truly startling aspect of the adoption of the 14th Amendment. As noted in Chapter 10, it was the effort of the anti-Federalists which caused the Bill of Rights to be adopted as a restraint on the power of the federal government. Accordingly, in 1833 Chief Justice Marshall in Barron v. Baltimore determined that the Bill of Rights did not apply to the states and that the 5th Amendment's prohibition against taking private property without just compensation was not binding on the states. They could take your property without just compensation. Forward then to 1897 when the same Supreme Court, in Quincy Railways vs. Chicago,[33] reversed Barron and held that states did indeed have to give you just compensation when they took your property. Well, how do you do, and how did that happen?

Wouldn't you know it? It was the 14th Amendment! The Court found that "due process" meant that the just compensation provision in the 5th Amendment did apply to the states. I suppose paying someone a fair price for their property could be considered "process" but it sounds pretty substantive to most people.

This began a long series of Supreme Court cases, which continue today, holding various provisions of the Bill of Rights to apply to the states through the Due Process Clause of the 14th Amendment. By way of example, here is a much abbreviated list:

- Freedom of speech, <u>Gitlow v. New York</u> (1925);
- Right to counsel in capital cases, <u>Powell v. Alabama</u> (1932);
- Ban on unreasonable searches and seizures, <u>Wolf v. Colorado</u> (1949);
- Right to counsel in all felony cases, <u>Gideon v. Wainwright</u> (1963);
- No double jeopardy, <u>Benton v. Maryland</u> (1968); and:
- The right to keep and bear arms, <u>McDonald v. Chicago</u> (2009).

In effect, the 14th Amendment has trumped the Bill of Rights. They were enacted to staunch the spread of federal power. Now the 14th Amendment has reversed that intent and put the states under the federal thumb. On the face of it, the two words "due process" don't seem to jump out at you and say this phrase was meant to bind the states to the substance of the prohibitions of the Bill of Rights. But, taking a broader view, it does make good political sense.

By 1897, when <u>Quincy Railways</u> was decided, America had grown so that it truly was from sea to shining sea. The Civil War was a couple of decades in the past and America began to think as one nation for the first time. Looking ahead the Supreme Court probably couldn't imagine a situation where basic civil rights varied wildly among the states. Uniformity seemed a good thing and the crack in the door that they went through was "due process." No surprise, the Court does seem to step into the political breach when it perceives that all else has failed. (Refer to Chapter 2).

ONE PERSON/ ONE VOTE AND THE 14th AMENDMENT

1964 was another milestone for the advancement of democracy in America. The Court advanced equality and fairness by requiring each state to be controlled by the principle of one person/ one vote.[34] This required all states be democratic Republics. The Court stated that the right to vote "is the essence of a democratic society, and any restrictions on the right strike at the heart of representative government." Just as important, it found that the *"debasement or dilution" of the vote can be just as effective as prohibiting the vote entirely.*

In the same year the Supreme Court also imposed on the House of Representatives the same one person/one vote requirement.[35] The Court's articulation of the premise of its decision is impressive:

"We do not believe that the Framers of the Constitution intended to permit the same vote-diluting discrimination to be accomplished through the device of districts containing widely varied numbers of inhabitants. To say that a vote is worth more in one district than in another would not only run counter to our fundamental ideas of democratic government, it would cast aside the principle of a House of Representatives elected 'by the People,' a principle tenaciously fought for and established at the Constitutional Convention."

The Court continued:

"No right is more precious in a free country than that of having a voice in the election of those who make the laws under which, as good citizens, we must live. Other rights, even the most basic, are illusory if the right to vote is undermined. Our Constitution leaves no room for classification of people in a way that unnecessarily abridges this right."

Justice Harlan dissented in both cases. He made a very interesting point. He observed that all of the arguments made by the majorities could apply equally to the Senate. What, he asked, about that? What indeed?

THE HOUSE AND THE 14th AMENDMENT

The Supreme Court's decision should have made the House of Representatives into a truly democratic body, and it would have were it not for gerrymandering. How can the gerrymander withstand the Court's language quoted above that "debasement or dilution" of the vote can be just as effective as prohibiting it in its entirety? That is the whole purpose of the gerrymander. It is the very definition of debasement. On its face it violates the 14th Amendment. It is unconstitutional—on the other hand, it is fixable![36]

THE SENATE AND THE 5th AND 14th AMENDMENTS

Consider what we have just seen. The Supreme Court overruled the purpose of the Bill of Rights and ignored the 10th Amendment to require all states to become democratic Republics. It then required all Congressional districts to have equal populations. Comes now the Senate, why is it sacrosanct?

Over the entrance to the Supreme Court building is inscribed:

"EQUAL JUSTICE UNDER LAW"

a value completely absent from the original Constitution!

Equality has become the seminal point in modern life. Whether gender, race or sexual orientation it is what drives our engines these days! But when it comes to the most important aspect of citizenship—*voting equality is denied.* Some citizens have not just twice the vote of another or three times the vote of another or 10 times the vote of another or 20 times or 30 times or 40 times or 50 times, but 55 times. The Supreme Court building should collapse under the weight of this totally unequal, unfair and disparate treatment.

It is all due to the structure of the Senate which is a holdover from a very undemocratic Republic. The disparity was born in the Connecticut Compromise which gave the states equality and denied it to the people. It contravenes the 14th Amendment's demand for equality.

The Founding Fathers lacked confidence in the ability of the governed to exercise the vote.[37] The 14th Amendment and Supreme Court now say otherwise. Everyone votes for everything. The Founding Fathers did not believe in equality and absolutely did not want universal suffrage. So long as the Senate remains in its present posture, equal protection on the federal level is meaningless! The Senate was created to be undemocratic and it is true to its origins. Its structure is comfortable with and consistent with an oligarchic Republic. It is completely inconsistent with the present demands of the 5th and 14th Amendments.

The Supreme Court has commented in passing on the Senate's disparate treatment of voting rights.[38] Referring to the Connecticut Compromise, it observed "each state including little Delaware and Rhode Island was to have two Senators. As a further guarantee that these Senators would be considered state emissaries, they were to be elected by the state legislatures, Article I, Section 3, and it was specially provided in Article V that no state should ever be deprived of its equal representation in the Senate."

Two things: first, since the passage of the 17th Amendment, Senators are no longer "emissaries of the states"; rather, they are emissaries of the people. And equal representation today means people, not states, one person/ one vote.

Second, the Court's observation quoted above deleted a very important part of Article V: The Court should have said that the states' equal representation couldn't be changed without their "*Consent.*" Amendments *change* and *improve* whatever had come before that is inconsistent. The states *consented* to and adopted the 5th Amendment with its Due Process Clause. It demands the same equal protection as the

14th Amendment, one person/ one vote. The 5th and the 14th Amendments trump Article V! It demands one person/ one vote. Let me explain.

The various meanings of amendments migrate over time. I don't want to go too far out on a limb, but I expect that what was on most people's minds at the time the 14th Amendment was ratified was the protection of former slaves. That is important to know but it is not controlling with respect to the present meaning of the Due Process and Equal Protection Clauses of that Amendment.

Still out on that limb, I expect that the folks in 1868 would have been shocked to learn that in today's world the 14th Amendment has been interpreted to:

- Bar jail time for a woman having an early-term abortion;
- Outlaw racial segregation in schools;
- Require states to provide free lawyers to indigent defendants in criminal trials;
- Cause the Bill of Rights to bind the states;
- Bar jail time for same sex relations;
- Require every state to demand one person/one vote;
- Bind the federal government through the Due Process Clause of the 5th Amendment, and:
- Sanction gay marriage.

The above decisions seem a bit removed from protecting former slaves. But to the point: the Supreme Court articulates in dramatic fashion how important it is that all citizens have equal voting rights—not diluted! The fact that the House is one person/one vote is meaningless until the Senate follows suit. It is akin to building a bridge halfway across the mighty Mississippi—great effort with a very bad result.

The 5th Amendment presently affords to federal citizens the same equal protection that the 14th Amendment provides to state citizens. How can an institution born in a time of slavery, when few citizens even had the vote, fail to yield to the demands of an amendment that based on all current case law gives our citizens a guarantee of equal voting rights? What is this idol we worship? How can this anachronistic hangover of a different age hamstring our government? Senators are not emissaries of the states! They represent the people.

To reiterate, the meanings of amendments migrate over time. The present meaning of the 5th Amendment is that all Americans are entitled to one person/one vote without dilution. The 5th Amendment was agreed to by the states when it was ratified in 1791. Accordingly, Article V must submit to the 5th Amendment's present meaning.

THE 5th AND 14th AMENDMENTS AND DEMOCRACY

California now has 55 House members. On the other hand, Wyoming has to count its bears to justify having even one. This means that in the Senate one vote in Wyoming has a California equivalent of 55. The 21 least populous states have roughly the same population as California, 37 million. In the Senate they have 42 votes and California has two. The 26 least populated states have approximately 20 percent of the U.S. population, and were it not for the filibuster, enough voting power to control the entire government. The nine most populous states have over 50 percent of the population and 18% of the votes.

There is no definition of democracy that has its eligible citizens with unequal voting power. Once you go down the road to having unequal voting, you are on your way to an oligarchy. And while there are several different types of democracies, there are distinguishing and required elements: equality and majority rule being foremost. In fact, they are the mirror image of one another, for without equality, the majority is simply a ruse. To have a legitimate majority, equality among the voters is necessary. Just having the vote doesn't create a democracy. All U.S. citizens are supposed to be equal before the law.

If you inquire how to justify the disparity in voting between California and Wyoming, the response is predictable: "That it is what the Founding Fathers intended." True enough. But they also intended that state legislators elect United States senators, that women and minorities not vote and that slavery be legal. They have been *overruled* by the 13th, 15th, 17th and 19th Amendments. They have also been overruled by the 5th and 14th Amendments guaranteeing everyone one person/one vote. This is not your grandfather's Constitution.

If, for example, we have 20 citizens, each with one vote but three of them have their votes counted six times, the result can be 18 to 17 with the three prevailing. This is the tyranny of the minority—because it is votes, not noses, which are counted.

The 5th and 14th Amendments demand democracy. If every vote must equal every other vote then, for the essential processes of government, the House, the Senate and voting for the President must operate by majority rule to comply with their demands. Obviously, if a minority vote controls, then each minority vote exceeds each majority vote, i.e., each of the 41 minority votes exceeds each of the 59 majority votes if the minority is to win. And the 5th and 14th Amendments did not exempt the Senate from their requirements. To be clear, equal protection, one person/ one vote and government by the few, an oligarchy, are *mutually exclusive.*

THE SENATE FAILS THE DEMANDS OF EQUAL PROTECTION ON TWO SEPARATE GROUNDS

First, it is still operating as if America is an undemocratic Republic, i.e., states are equal and people are not.

Second, the Senate also fails due to the filibuster. The filibuster is not part of the Constitution and, until recently, may not have arisen to the level of Constitutional scrutiny as it was rarely used. Now, however, it has become a part of the regular business of the Senate and by rule 41 votes can stop the government from functioning. Like the gerrymander, the sole purpose of the filibuster is to create unequal voting rights.

Filibuster, by the way, means "pirate." [39] So if there was a boat waiting at the end of that bridge that was built halfway across the mighty Mississippi, it would do no good as it has been commandeered by pirates.

For the pirate to take over these days, all that is needed is the threat he will arrive! Presently the 21 least populous states have 42 votes and can, by rule, stop the government from operating. Those 42 votes potentially represent 13 percent of the population, roughly the same as California. So it is possible for the pirate to arrive and the popular vote be 40 million no, 265 million yes, and the noes have it in America, the democracy. And while the filibuster has been set aside for routine executive appointments and federal judges other than the Supreme Court, it remains in place for all legislation and the Supreme Court.

Without more, the form of the Senate prevents our Constitution from being a democracy. Majorities don't rule and our citizens' votes are not equal. It deprives all of us of the equal protection guaranteed to us by the 5th and 14th Amendments. Equality is essential to justice.

THE ELECTORAL COLLEGE

The electoral process for the election of the President of the United States is driven by the fact that the loser of the popular vote can be the winner of the election. It constitutes one more barrier to our democracy, one person/one vote. What kind of perverse rule has the loser of the popular vote for our most important election, the President, win and still call ourselves a democracy?

The Supreme Court's decision in Bush v. Gore[40] is particularly interesting in this respect:

"Having once granted the right to vote on equal terms the state may *not*, by later arbitrary or disparate treatment, *value one person's vote over that of another*."

The Court in its analysis of the vote in Florida gets into the micro details of counting hanging chads (the little piece of paper that is punched out when you vote) and finds that there was "an unequal valuation of ballots in various respects."

The Court was analyzing one person's handling of a chad versus another's handling of a chad. It concluded that this was a violation of the Equal Protection Clause of the 14th

Amendment, one ballot to another, because the same chad might be seen differently by different people.

The Court's reasoning is based in part upon the Electoral College and the ability of state legislatures to turn the selection of the electors over to the direct vote of the people. The Electoral College is provided for in the 12th Amendment which states in part:

> "The electors…shall name in their ballots the person voted for as President, and in distinct ballots the person voted for as Vice President, and they shall make distinct lists of all persons voted for as President, and for all persons voted for as Vice President, and for the number of votes for each, which lists they shall sign and certify…"

It anticipates that there will be many different "persons voted for" for each—the President and the Vice President. The history of the Electoral College is that the Founding Fathers didn't trust the state legislatures to elect the President and created a further baffle, the Electoral College. As indicated by the language ("all persons voted for") of the 12th Amendment and by history, the electors were intended to exercise their own individual opinions as to for whom to vote for President:

> "And so the debate went, until someone suggested creating an alternative Congress of independent electors that would have the sole and exclusive responsibility for electing the President every four years. Thus the Electoral College was born….The states could select their electors in any way they chose, and the electors were free to vote for any two people they wished, as long as one of them was from outside the state." [41]

There is still a sense in America that this is so, that the electors can vote for whom they please. Nevertheless, 48 states, whether by statute, required pledge or practice, dictate that the electors vote "winner takes all." Two states, Maine and Nebraska, have their own peculiar requirements.

The sense of the people probably reflects the obvious: If the state legislatures can direct the vote of the Electoral College, what possible reason is there to have the Electoral College to begin with? If the legislature can control the Electoral College, why wouldn't the Founding Fathers simply have had the state legislatures do the voting in the first place? The state legislatures directing the Electoral College has to be unconstitutional.

Nevertheless, the practice of the state legislatures directing the Electoral College is long-standing and pervasive. So if we accept the practice, to be consistent with its own reasoning, the Supreme Court in <u>Bush v. Gore</u> should have found that the "winner takes all" provision is unconstitutional.

If on the *micro* level unequal treatment of ballots was unconstitutional, how then on the *macro* level can the states simply refuse to count 50 percent (less one vote) of the votes cast? This clearly "values one person's vote over that of another." The "winner takes all" means that half the votes aren't counted. How can discounting 50% (less 1 vote) to 0 be consistent with the underlying reasoning of <u>Bush v. Gore</u>? The state legislature of Florida directed half the votes not be counted!

In a democracy the only way a state legislature could direct the Electoral College vote would have to be consistent with the popular vote. If the winner gets 54 percent of the votes, then 54 percent of the electors must vote that way and 46 percent vote for the loser, otherwise it isn't equal protection, one person/one vote, consistent with the 5th and 14th Amendments.

MINORITY CONTROL

We have now seen that all of the essential parts of the legislative and executive branches are subject to control by minority voting. Since when is minority control democratic? Our present form of government is *not democratic*. Nine states have half the population and 18 percent of the vote and everything has to clear the Senate where states are equal and citizens are not. Given the pirates, the percentage gets even worse. The great urban areas of America are essentially without representation on the federal level. Dallas, Houston, Miami, Philadelphia, New York, Chicago, San Francisco and

Los Angeles can be stalemated by Wyoming, Montana, North and South Dakota, Vermont and Alaska. *There is no articulable rational basis for this that is consistent with democracy and equal protection.*

To repeat, we have a Constitution made up of the original Constitution plus 27 Amendments. It is all just one Constitution. Historically it has been changed piece by piece and now lies in pieces. It is just an assemblage of unrelated rules. It has within it the oligarchic Republic framed by the Founding Fathers—the Senate—and the democracy required by the 5th and 14th Amendments, totally separate theories of government.

THE ASCENDANCE OF THE 14th AMENDMENT

A much larger point is that the "Cry" of the last half century is for equality in all of its forms. Central to the clamor for equality is the 14th Amendment and its progeny. Its importance is staggering. Brown v. Board is a decision that helped lead to the enactment of the Civil Rights Act of 1964 and the Voting Rights Act of 1965 all of which are monuments in the racial transition of America leading to the advancement of equality and due process for all of its citizens. Then came the Supreme Court's decisions requiring one person/one vote. The fight for equality for women, gays and minority populations has been based on the 14th Amendment and all that it has spawned.

WHAT IS LEFT OF THE ORIGINAL CONSTITUTION?

Has the original Constitution been supplanted? The following analysis suggests that may be the case.

A. Originally the House of Representatives was intended to be elected by a small group of well-to-do white men, including slave owners. The House is now elected by universal suffrage, not a distinction without a difference. It changes the very makeup of the House from white men to men and women of all races and religions with different cultures and values. Further, the House no longer has districts with unequal populations. On the other hand, it is largely controlled by gerrymandering, a practice not included in the original Constitution, and that continues to allow minority control. The House no longer functions as the old Republic but rather as a gerrymandered democracy.

B. The Senate, like the House, is now elected by universal suffrage, not as originally provided, by the various state legislatures. As a result, Senators now represent the people, not the states. Accordingly, it has a different constituent makeup, less diverse than the House, but nevertheless different by culture and character than that intended by the Founding Fathers. It continues to act as the old Republic in the teeth of the 5th and 14th Amendments.

Finally, it has adopted the filibuster as a regular part of its proceedings in violation of the 5th and 14th Amendments and majority control.

C. The President is no longer elected by the Electoral College as intended by the 12th Amendment, but potentially by a minority of the popular vote contrary to the majority rule originally called for. "Winner Takes All" discounts to 0 one-half (less one vote) of the votes cast, in violation of the 5th and 14th Amendments, the Supreme Court and the 12th Amendment.

D. As to the presidency, it has effectively assumed the War Power from Congress and many of the prerogatives of foreign policy without the consent of Congress. Additionally, through "Signing Statements" the presidency has indicated that the office may be above the law and has in many instances disregarded the law with impunity.

E. The Bill of Rights now applies as restrictions on the states.

F. Slavery has been abolished.

G. Universal suffrage has been extended to age 18.

H. The Electoral College is controlled by the state legislatures.

I. Minority voting controls the House and Senate and potentially the election of the President.

J. A potential lifetime presidency has been abolished.

K. One person/one vote and equal protection have been adopted as our governing principles and applied to the state and federal governments through the 5th and 14th Amendments and Article I, Section 2, of the Constitution.

L. Separation of powers is suspect due to the assumption of the War Power by the presidency and presidential signing statements.

M. The Constitution is now nominally a democracy but in fact is neither a democracy nor an oligarchic Republic, just a collection of unrelated rules allowing minority voting to control the government.

N. All states must be democratic Republics.

A review of the above list indicates that the original Constitution is on life support. Originalists have nothing much left to interpret. Indeed, even the idea of "Original Intent" contravenes reality. There are as many original intents as there are negotiators in any transaction, including the Constitution.

CONCLUSION

We call ourselves a democracy. We purport to act by majority vote. We do not. This is true even though our institutions of government are set up to work that way. Except for the two-third votes required for treaties, impeachment, overriding vetoes and constitutional amendments, the Constitution assumes all the other functions of government will be done by majority vote. In fact, the House and Senate act as though that is the rule. If it were true, stalemates would disappear because majority rule effects decision-making.

Decisions prove themselves. Even wrong decisions are often better than no decisions since they 1) establish that decision-making is possible; and, therefore, 2) can be corrected. Both Apple and Coca-Cola have demonstrated this in the not too distant past. Heat seeking missiles are off course most of the time but eventually hit the target.

With majority rule, every vote counts and equality is achieved. Moreover, responsibility is apparent. Those making consistently wrong decisions can be removed.

On the other hand, *minority control has no father*, it is a placeholder for incumbency. Minority control has come to mean no decisions. This is a bureaucrat's heaven. No decisions means no bad decisions. No bad decisions means re-election. And re-election is the goal of every House and Senate vote.

Senators from sparsely populated states assert that minority control is somehow better. Why? What is it that suggests that control exercised by a minority will be wiser, more fair or more inclusive than one controlled by a majority? Isn't a majority, by its very nature, more inclusive? It is easy to define, 51% of all citizens. How do you define a minority? 41% of whom? Or 13% of whom? Or perhaps just one person, the complete minority, the one fellow chosen by the Army? Control is control. Tyranny, whether by the majority or minority, is allayed and individual liberties are protected by the Constitution itself, the Bill of Rights and the 14th Amendment in particular.

In any event, we now have a failure of government on a grand scale, a government controlled by minority voting, one founded upon an original Constitution that was profoundly un-democratic. The original Constitution has now been supplanted in nearly every respect by Supreme Court decisions, practice, and constitutional amendments, particularly the 14th. Of great weight is the conflict between the original Republic and the 5th and 14th Amendments. They demand equality and equality is essential to justice.

What now? Well, why not try to live up to our billing and become a democracy?!

1. The House: Demand the House restructure without gerrymanders and fix it.[42]

2. The Senate: Adjust the voting machine in the Senate to reflect the same number as the House members from each state, e.g., when a Senator from California votes, 55 pops up and when the Senator from Wyoming votes, 1 pops up. This just reverses the weight of votes presently extant in the Senate.

3. The Pirate: Hang him from the yardarm.

4. The President: Have the electors vote as a reflection of the popular vote, that is, if the popular vote is 54% to 46%, the Electoral College votes 54% to 46%.

FINALE
In the meantime, in a "democracy":
Having a voter disparity of 55 to 1 is ridiculous;
Having the gerrymander legal is ridiculous;
Having a Senate where 41 votes can beat 59 votes is ridiculous;
Having as little as 13% of the population able to prevent the government from operating is ridiculous;
Having the loser of the popular vote be the winner in an election for the presidency is ridiculous;
Believing that any of this will ever change is ridiculous;
and calling this a democracy is preposterous!

"You've been around here longer than I have. What are 'congressional ethics'?"

Chapter 9

Zero Tolerance
(Or Home Plate for Knuckleheads)

INTELLIGENCE AND JUDGMENT

There are two human qualities that most all of us admire, intelligence and judgment. Occasionally they get together in the same person, but not often enough. There are many very intelligent people who seem to lack any common sense, otherwise known as judgment. On the other hand, there are quite a number of people with very good judgment who are not particularly intelligent. As between the two, when we need good advice, we seek out the people we know who have good judgment irrespective of their I.Q.

No doubt good judgment is one of the most admired of all human qualities. When people are hired, one of the most sought-after qualities is good judgment. We hope that all of our leaders, our teachers, and our clergy are people of good judgment and we expect to find it in our judges, our military leaders and top politicians. As people age, it is called wisdom.

ZERO TOLERANCE

So who in the world came up with the idea of zero tolerance? It calls for us to abandon all judgment. Zero tolerance for drugs at school results in a second grader being sent home for having an aspirin in his pocket. No joke. It recalls Dante's exhortation: "Abandon all hope ye who enter here!" When you have surrendered one of the most precious of all human qualities, the one for which you may have been hired—good judgment—stupid and avoidable and bad things will happen, for you have become a total **KNUCKLEHEAD**, a person without judgment.

* * *

"How very exciting! I have never before met a <u>Second</u> Amendment lawyer."

Chapter 10

Ten Constitutional Restrictions

(Or What the Federal Government Cannot Do)

For the first time since our Constitution was adopted in 1788 the Supreme Court, in the case of The District of Columbia v. Heller,[43] has held that the 2nd Amendment of the Bill of Rights contains a constitutional right to "keep and carry" a gun. The holding of the case, as stated by the Reporter of Decisions, is that "the Second Amendment protects an individual right to *possess* a firearm unconnected with service in a militia, and to use that arm for traditionally lawful purposes, such as self-defense within the home." Or as stated by the Court:

"Like most rights, the right secured by the Second Amendment is not unlimited. From Blackstone through the

19th century cases, commentators and courts routinely explained that the right was not a *right to keep and carry* any weapon whatsoever in any manner whatsoever and for whatever purpose.... Although we do not undertake an exhaustive historical analysis today of the full scope of the Second Amendment, nothing in our opinion should be taken to cast doubt on longstanding prohibitions on the *possession of firearms* by felons and the mentally ill, or laws forbidding the carrying of firearms in sensitive places such as schools and government buildings, or laws imposing conditions and qualifications on the commercial sale of arms....

"We also recognize another important limitation on the right to *keep and carry* arms. Miller said, as we have explained, that the sorts of weapons protected were those 'in common use at the time'.[44] We think that limitation is fairly supported by the historical tradition of prohibiting the carrying of 'dangerous and unusual weapons'".[45]

In other words, there is a constitutional right for *certain people to keep and carry certain types of guns for certain purposes*. The Court's decision, which is 64 pages in length, was written by Justice Scalia. He also authored—what is either a long essay or a short treatise—"A Matter of Interpretation."[46] It is a wide-ranging commentary on the whole subject of judicial interpretation, including his approach to interpreting statutes and constitutional texts. He considers himself a textualist. He states that "when the text of a statute is clear, that is the end of the matter."[47] He is highly critical of ever considering legislative intent.[48] "The text is the law, and it is the text that must be observed."[49] "...a text should not be construed strictly, and it should not be construed leniently; it should be construed reasonably, to contain all that it fairly means."[50] In other words, the Goldilocks rule, you know, not too hot, not too cold, j-u-u-u-st right! One might expect that a Justice following that rule would come out somewhere in the middle, not too far to the right, not too far to the left. How has that worked out?

When considering interpreting constitutional texts he quotes Chief Justice Marshall's decision in <u>McCulloch vs. Maryland</u>[51] as the gold standard: "Chief Justice Marshall puts the point as well as it can be put."[52] Justice Scalia paraphrases Marshall: "In textual interpretation, context is everything, and the context of the Constitution tells us not to expect nitpicking detail, and to give words and phrases an expansive rather than a narrow interpretation—though not an interpretation that the language will not bear."[53] Interpreting constitutional text, Scalia gives great weight to the original meaning of the text.[54]

Who then could be a better source of the original intent of the Bill of Rights than Chief Justice Marshall himself?

In <u>Barron v. Baltimore</u>[55] he did just that. The plaintiff in that case had its private property taken by the City of Baltimore without having been paid "just compensation." The plaintiff contended that the provision of the 5th Amendment requiring just compensation when taking private property applied to the states. As stated by Marshall for the Court:

"The question thus presented is, we think, of great importance, but not of much difficulty. The Constitution was ordained and established by the people of the United States for themselves, for their own government, and not for the *government of the individual states*. Each state established a constitution for itself, and in that constitution provided such limitations and restrictions on the powers of its particular government as its judgment dictated. The people of the United States framed such a government for the United States as they supposed best adapted to their situation and best calculated to promote their interests. The powers they conferred on this government were to be exercised by itself, and the limitations on power, if expressed in general terms, are naturally, and we think necessarily, applicable to the government created by the instrument. They *are limitations of power granted in the instrument itself*, not of distinct governments framed by different persons and for the different purposes."[56]

Chief Justice Marshall continues: "But it is universally

understood, it is part of the history of the day, that the great revolution which established the Constitution of the United States was not effected without an immense opposition. Serious fears were extensively entertained that those powers which the patriot statesmen who then watched over the interests of our country deemed essential to the union, and to the attainment of those invaluable objects for which union was sought, might be exercised in a manner dangerous to liberty. In almost every convention by which the Constitution was adopted, *amendments to guard against the abuse of power* were recommended. These amendments demanded security against the apprehended encroachments of the General Government—*not against those of the local governments.* In compliance with a sentiment thus generally expressed, to quiet fears thus extensively entertained, amendments were proposed by the required majority in Congress and adopted by the states. These amendments contain no expression indicating an intention to apply them to the state governments. This court cannot so apply them.

"We are of the opinion that the provision in the Fifth Amendment to the Constitution declaring that private property shall not be taken for public use without just compensation is intended solely as a limitation on the exercise of power by the government of the United States, *and is not applicable to the legislation of the States.*"[57]

One other comment of the Court in the <u>Barron</u> case is worth noting:

"…the Fifth Amendment must be understood as restraining the power of the General Government, not as applicable to the States."[58]

The actual holding of the case then is that the State of Maryland could take your private property without just compensation. In other words, the states' powers were *plenary.*

Chief Justice Marshall's opinion reflects that at the time of the adoption of the Constitution in 1788 there were many who were quite concerned about the potential expansion of power of the new Federal Government. They were the Anti-Federalists.

They were strenuously opposed by the Federalists, which included James Madison. To accomplish their purposes the Anti-Federalists proposed many, in fact hundreds, of amendments to restrict the power of the new government. This bit of history is well described by Professor Wood in his contribution to the *Oxford History of the United States* entitled *Empire of Liberty.*[59] Professor Wood notes that: "The Philadelphia Convention had not seriously considered adding to the Constitution a Bill of Rights that would restrict the power of the national government." He goes on to say that the Federalists (the Philadelphia Conventionalists) believed that the Bill of Rights would dilute the power of the national government and that they were determined to resist all efforts to add amendments. He analogizes it to the Magna Carta of 1215 "limiting the King's prerogative."

Madison finally came around to supporting a few select amendments. He sifted through hundreds and reduced them to twelve. Ten were finally ratified in 1791 and as stated by Professor Wood, "The American Bill of Rights of 1791 was less a creative document than a defensive one…. The American Bill of Rights was simply part of the familiar English customary law that work to limit pre-existing governmental power."[60] And while Madison's preamble to the Bill of Rights was not adopted, it is nevertheless good evidence of intent:

> "The Conventions of a number of the *States* having at the time of their adopting of the Constitution, expressed a desire, in order to prevent misconstruction or abuse of its powers, that further declaratory and *restrictive clauses* should be added…." (Preamble to the Bill of Rights).

The 9th and 10th Amendments themselves confirm this intent. The 9th protects the rights retained by the people from any interpretation of the Constitution which would disparage those rights. Similarly the 10th reserved to the states all powers not specifically delegated to the United States. Both reaffirm the restrictive nature of the Bill of Rights.

In summary, the Bill of Rights was a statement of a bargained relationship between the new Federal Government and the states that ratified the Constitution with the understanding that it would be amended to protect the states and the people from expanding federal power. They outlined what the Federal Government *couldn't* do, for example, take your property without just compensation, and what the states *could* do, for example, take your property without paying just compensation. *It is a list of restrictions rather than a grant of rights.*

Consider the scene described by Chief Justice Marshall. He reflects that in each of the conventions leading up to the adoption of the Constitution protests were made against its adoption without putting limits on its power. The *Founders opposed* these amendments. Hundreds were proposed and Madison was able to negotiate them down to twelve. Imagine the arguments back and forth over getting the agreement of Madison and the rest of the other Founders to language which would restrict their hard-fought-for new government. This was at a time when state sovereignty was much greater than today. As mentioned by Marshall, each state had its own constitutional limits. No doubt the scriveners were hard at work fighting over each word of the new restrictions that would comprise the new Bill of Rights.

Remember what we are dealing with: Fourteen sovereignties, the Federal Government and 13 states that were sovereign in ways we can't imagine today. The United States of 1800 was united only on paper and the paper was the Constitution. It took 100 years, the Civil War, and the Supreme Court to bring them together as a nation. (Refer to Chapter 1).

THE 2nd AMENDMENT

The 2nd Amendment reads:

"A well-regulated Militia, being necessary to the security of a free state, the right of the people to keep and bear Arms shall not be infringed."

The drafters understood this to restrict the power of the government created by the new Constitution. Read that way, rather than as a grant of rights, the Second Amendment has only *one obvious meaning:* The Federal Government could not interfere with the right of the state to have a well-regulated militia by infringing on the right of the state's people to keep and bear arms—or stated another way—the Federal Government could not infringe on the right of the state's people to keep and bear arms as a way of preventing the state from having a well-regulated militia. The point of the amendment is that the states wanted to ensure that they could have a well-regulated militia and that the Federal Government couldn't interfere with that right by taking away the state's people's right to keep and bear arms. It has absolutely nothing to do with the right of the state to regulate guns or to have a militia.

Under Barron, a state could take your property without paying for it. That is more than perplexing. Think what you might call a state or nation that did that today. A dictatorship? Remember, the Founders were not democrats, very few people could vote, there was no provision for equality, slavery was legal and a state could take your property without paying for it. But states couldn't regulate guns? Really? They could probably take your guns without paying for them. No doubt they could abolish their militia, infringe on the right of the people to keep and bear arms, form a state religion, try you twice for the same crime or conduct searches without a warrant. They had plenary power.

Returning then to the meaning of the 2nd Amendment, "Arms" are defined by the *Oxford English Dictionary* (OED) as "defensive and offensive outfit for war, things used in fighting" and "instruments of offense used in war; weapons. By arms, we understand those instruments of offense generally made use of in war...." The time cited, 1794, is right at the heart of the time to test original intent. Further, the OED defines "to bear arms" as "to serve as a soldier, do military service, fight."[61]

Given that Justice Scalia follows the Goldilocks rule and that the purpose of the 2nd Amendment is to support the continuity of a well-regulated militia, there should be no doubt about what "bearing arms" would mean. Curiously, the Court found a right to "keep and carry" rather than a right to "own" a weapon or firearm. To explain: the court always chooses its words carefully There is no definition of the word "keep" that means "own." There are no synonyms for the word "keep" that means "own." Question: Was the concept of a constitutional right to actually own weaponry just a step too far for the Court? And why "keep and carry" rather than "keep and bear?" Did the latter sound just a bit too militaristic?

One thing is clear: The Supreme Court did not find that there was a constitutional right to "own" a weapon or firearm.

Justice Scalia's understanding of the origins of the Bill of Rights is, as he put it in describing Justice Stevens' dissent in Heller,[62] "dead wrong." His view:

"So also, we value the right to bear arms less than did the Founders (who thought the right of self-defense to be absolutely fundamental), and there will be few tears shed if and when the Second Amendment is held to guarantee nothing more than the state National Guard. But this just shows that the Founders were right when they feared that some (in their view misguided) future generation might wish to abandon liberties that they *considered* essential, *and so sought to protect those liberties in a Bill of Rights.* We may *like* the abridgment of property rights and *like* the elimination of the right to bear arms; but let us not pretend that these are not *reductions* of *rights.*"[63]

He sees the Bill of Rights, and the 2nd Amendment in particular, as a grand scheme of the Founders to bestow rights on the people. In fact, as set forth by Justice Marshall, the Bill of Rights was *opposed* by the Founders. The Bill of Rights served only to restrict the power of the new federal government, not to grant rights to "protect liberties." Wrong again. The states would define what liberties their people had.

The Justice continues:

"If the courts are free to write the Constitution anew, they will, by God, write it the way the majority wants; the appointment and confirmation process will see to that. This, of course, is the end of the Bill of Rights, whose meaning will be committed to the very body it was meant to protect against: the majority. By trying to make the Constitution do everything that needs doing from age to age, we shall have caused it to do nothing at all."[64]

What he is saying is that he fears that the political appointment process will bring people onto the Court who disagree with him and that they will write the Constitution anew. It seems as though he fits that description perfectly. He sees the Bill of Rights as written to prevent the "majority" from taking away rights from the "minority," rather than what they were intended for: To protect the states and their people from an invasion of their rights by the federal government. Wrong again.

But given his view he must find a way around the obvious: that "keep and bear arms," using the Goldilocks rule, simply means supporting a militia. Accordingly, it takes 64 pages of parsing words and arguing with Justice Stephens to justify his view that the 2nd Amendment guarantees certain people the right to keep and carry certain weapons for certain kinds of purposes.

But enough of that, back to Justice Scalia's decision. He sets forth, as far as it goes, a fair reading of the 2nd Amendment: "Because a well-regulated militia is necessary to the security of a free state, the right of the people to keep and bear arms shall not be infringed."[65] What he leaves out is, *by the Federal Government.* The state was, of course, free to do the infringing.

With respect to finding non-military definitions for the phrase "keep and bear arms," the Justice struggled.

"These provisions demonstrate—again, in the most analogous linguistic context—that 'bear arms' was *not limited* to the carrying of arms in a militia.[66]

"Of course, as we have said, the fact that the phrase was commonly used in a particular context does not show that it is limited to that context, and, in any event, we have given many sources where the phrase was used in nonmilitary contexts.[67]

"And even if 'keep and bear Arms' were a unitary phrase, we find no evidence that it bore a military meaning. Although the phrase was not at all common (which would be unusual for a term of art), we have found instances of its use with a clearly nonmilitary connotation."[68]

He is clearly not following the Goldilocks rule here. The Justice stretches to make the exceptions into the rule while straining to undo 220 years of judicial restraint. And what happened to being a textualist?

Towards the end of the opinion the Justice writes: "As the quotations earlier in this opinion demonstrate, the inherent right of self-defense has been central to the Second Amendment right."[69] He makes the same point in "A Matter of Interpretation." The Founders "thought the right of self-defense to be absolutely fundamental."[70] If so, why wasn't "self-defense" in the Bill of Rights, or better yet, Article I, Section 10, of the Constitution? In any event, as I read the text of the 2nd Amendment ("and it is the text that must be observed" per Scalia),[71] I don't see anything in there about "self-defense." Question: How do those quotations differ from his forbidden "legislative intent?"

ONE LAST THOUGHT

How can an amendment, adopted to restrict federal power, be interpreted to have morphed into a new federal right? Anyone? Seriously, anyone?

THE 2nd AMENDMENT AND THE DISTRICT OF COLUMBIA

The 2nd Amendment requires that the federal government not interfere with a state's right to have a militia. The last time I checked, the District of Columbia was not a state and never had a militia. How is the 2nd Amendment involved? The District of Columbia is nothing more than the United States government. So far as I know, the federal government is in no way restricted with respect to the regulation of guns in the

District of Columbia. Or Puerto Rico. Or Guam. Or Yosemite, for that matter.

THE 2nd AMENDMENT AND THE DUE PROCESS CLAUSE

Two years after its decision in <u>Heller</u>, the Supreme Court applied the same rule to the states through the Due Process Clause of the 14th Amendment in the case of <u>McDonald v. Chicago</u>.[72] By way of explanation, let's look again at <u>Barron</u> which is cited in <u>McDonald</u>. Recall that it held that while the federal government was prohibited by the 5th Amendment from taking one's property without just compensation, the state *could* take your property without just compensation. And as set forth above, the 2nd Amendment clearly prohibits the federal government from infringing the right of the people to keep and bear arms as a way of keeping the state from having a well-regulated militia. However, after the adoption of the 14th Amendment in 1868, the Supreme Court began to look at one of its provisions—no *state* could "deprive any person of life, liberty, or property, without due process of law" as a way of requiring states to be restricted in the same manner that the federal government had been restricted. That was accomplished by an interpretation of "Due Process" to include substance, not just process. Accordingly, states would now be required to pay just compensation when taking private property. The Court in <u>McDonald</u> held that such a reading of the Due Process Clause bound the states to the 2nd Amendment in the same manner that the federal government had been bound by it.

It turns out the 2nd Amendment is unique among the amendments in the Bill of Rights. The first eight amendments deal with specific rights that the federal government cannot invade. Only the 2nd Amendment deals with a right of a state, as opposed to the rights of the people, which are dealt with in the other seven. Take, for example, the right of the state to take your property without just compensation. Given the Supreme Court's interpretation of the Due Process Clause, it now puts the state in the same position as the federal government. The state will now be required to pay just compensation to its citizens.

But the 2nd Amendment is different. It is the right of the state not to be interfered with by the federal government. The Due Process Clause would then mean the state can't prevent *itself* from interfering with its own right to have a well-regulated militia by depriving the people of their right to keep and bear arms. It makes no sense. Presumably any state could abolish its own militia any time it saw fit.

It seems as though the Supreme Court stopped reading Barron immediately after Chief Justice Marshall's statement, "The question thus presented is, we think, of great importance, but not of much difficulty." Without reading the full text, the court comes away with the view that the only holding in Barron is that the Bill of Rights requires the federal government to pay just compensation when taking private property, but does not bind the states. What the Court seems to miss is that this leaves the states with plenary power and that they can take your property without just compensation and do anything else their Constitutions might allow, including declaring a state religion, trying you twice for the same crime or regulating guns.

Strange that in two cities, Washington, D.C., and Chicago, where there has been, and continues to be, outrageous gun violence, the Supreme Court sees fit to change 220 years of precedent to deny the states the ability to deal with their own problems and protect their citizens.

JUSTICE SCALIA AND THE DUE PROCESS CLAUSE

In *A Matter of Interpretation* Justice Scalia also sets forth his view on the subject of the Due Process Clause and its ability to incorporate against the states the *substance* of the prohibitions contained in the Bill of Rights:

"Well, it may or may not be a good thing to guarantee additional liberties, but the Due Process Clause quite obviously does not bear that interpretation. By its inescapable terms it guarantees *only process*. Property can be taken by the state; liberty can be taken; even life can be taken; but not without the *process* that our traditions require—notably, a validly enacted law and a fair trial. To say otherwise is to abandon textualism, and to render democratically adopted texts mere springboards for judicial lawmaking."[73]

His point seems well taken. Process is procedure and substance is not. Therefore, incorporating substance through a process clause seems inappropriate. He goes on to say:

"The basic linguistic point that 'substantive due process' [is] an oxymoron

...has great force....

"If I believed that 'due process' meant 'due substance' when the Fourteenth Amendment was adopted, I certainly would not feel free to abandon that meaning simply because nowadays we aspire to avoid words that mean the opposite of what they say....

"Of course I do not believe it."[74]

Justice Scalia wrote a concurring opinion in <u>McDonald v. Chicago</u>. Having previously declared that he rejects Substantive Due Process, his concurring opinion is more interesting than ever:

"I join the Court's opinion. Despite my misgivings about substantive due process as an original matter, I have acquiesced in the Court's incorporation of certain *guarantees* in the Bill of Rights 'because it is both long *established* and *narrowly limited.*' "[75]

Guarantees? They weren't guarantees, they were restrictions. "Long established?" Substantive due process is a new kid on the block compared to the right of the states, under their plenary power, to regulate guns any way they saw fit for 220 years. His declaration that he doesn't *"believe"* in substantive due process has now become *"misgivings."* And "narrowly limited"? Substantive due process has, in effect, completely reversed the meaning of the Bill of Rights. Amendments enacted to keep the federal government out of the business of the states have now been interpreted, through the

Due Process Clause, to control the states. The states have been put under the federal thumb.

Justice Scalia abandoned his strongly-held belief that substantive due process is an oxymoron that he does not believe in, in order to achieve his pre-ordained result. Goldilocks is dead. Had he followed his previously stated beliefs, the case would have gone the other way.

SUMMARY AND CONCLUSION

There have been heated debates for many years over the meaning of the wording of the 2nd Amendment. The arguments have been premised on the assumption that the Bill of Rights was adopted by the Founding Fathers to grant us certain inalienable rights. The problem? That just isn't true. As we have seen from the decision of Chief Justice Marshall in the case of <u>Barron v. Baltimore</u> and from Professor Gordon Wood's excellent history of that period, *Empire of Liberty*, the Bill of Rights was adopted as the result of a negotiation between the states and the new federal government. The states, led by the anti-federalists, feared the expanding power of the new nation. Accordingly, they proposed amendments as assurances against that prospect. The Founding Fathers actually opposed the adoption of these restrictive amendments. James Madison finally negotiated hundreds of proposals down to twelve, ten of which we're finally adopted and called the Bill of Rights. Those were rights created for the states and their people against the new federal government. Amendments 9 and 10 are particularly instructive in this respect. Amendment 9 reads:

> "The enumeration in the Constitution of certain rights shall not be construed to deny or disparage others retained by the people."

On its face this amendment is a restriction on the Constitution limiting its interpretation in favor of the people. Amendment 10 reads:

> "The powers not delegated to the United States by the Constitution, nor prohibited by it to the States, are reserved to the States respectively, or to the people."

Once again, this amendment on its face restricts the power of the new federal government.

These two amendments confirm what we learn from Chief Justice Marshall and from Gordon Wood and from history that the Bill of Rights was adopted to be and should be read as restrictions on the federal government. Read that way the 2nd Amendment can only mean one thing: the federal government can't jeopardize the ability of the states to have well-regulated militias by taking away the people's right to bear arms.

At the same time the states all retained their sovereignty and were limited only by their own constitutions, which may or may not provide for any gun rights. Or as stated by Chief Justice Marshall:

"Each state established a constitution for itself, and in that constitution provided such limitations and restrictions on the powers of its particular government as its judgment dictated."

Two final notes about Justice Scalia's gun rights decisions. The Heller case was brought by the District of Columbia, which is not a state. The Second Amendment has no application to it. And in the McDonald case he abandoned the fact that he does not believe in substantive due process in order to achieve his desired result. Taken together or separately these two decisions stand him in good stead for the **KNUCKLEHEAD** award.

In conclusion, both the Heller and McDonald decisions were wrongly decided based upon the history and intent of the Bill of Rights. They are simply political decisions, as is more clearly described in Chapter 2 of this book.

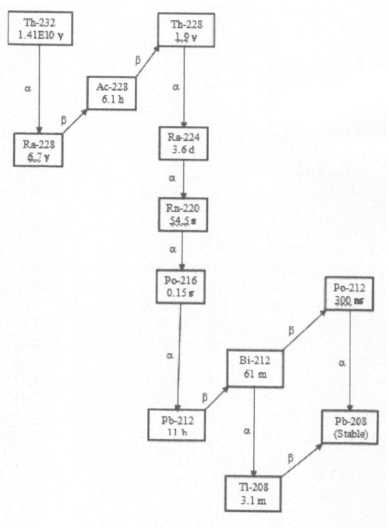

A decay scheme leading to stable lead.

Chapter 11

The Half-Life of Lead
(Or Know Your Risk)

Not long after the tragedies of 9/11 an expert on terrorism appeared on the Lehrer News Hour. He (I will call him Mr. Jones) was terrific. He discussed nearly every possible aspect of terrorism including nuclear, biological, chemical, car bombs and you name it, he covered the field. Obviously impressed Lehrer asked, "And so, Mr. Jones, how do you suggest we protect ourselves?" "Two things," he responded: "Don't smoke and wear your seatbelts!" Yes, indeed, we need to keep our eyes on the real risks in life. The person who is most likely to kill us is the one we see in the mirror in the morning.

Which brings us to the half-life of lead. For all practical purposes it is a stable element. Thus, it has no recognizable half-life. On the other hand, lead is very toxic and can be found everywhere—in your home, at your office, in the environment, in your food, and in the air. Scientists have never been able to find a dose so small that it is not harmful to you. You may want to keep that in mind if you happen to live in one of the handful of towns in America named Lead or Leadville or Galena (a mineral composed of lead and sulfur). To repeat—no dosage is so small that it is not harmful to you! Keep an eye on those real risks.

Unlike lead there are certain elements that do have half-lives because they are radioactive—meaning that they have nuclei that break down, emitting radiation. Accordingly, they decay over time. The rate of decay is measured in half-lives or the amount of time it takes for one-half of their nuclei to decay. Depending on the dose and type, radiation is harmful to human health.

One of the best-known of the radioactive elements is uranium 238. It has a half-life of 4.5 billion years, the age of the earth. On the other hand, the half-life of another radioactive element, iodine 131, is eight days. It is important to understand that for a comparable amount of material, iodine 131 is much more dangerous than uranium 238 since in a shorter period of time it will emit much more radiation. Obviously the longer the half-life, the slower radiation is emitted.

Just like lead, radioactivity is everywhere. You may want to know that the next time you eat a banana you will be ingesting radioactive potassium 40, which has a half-life of 1.3 billion years. And every one of us contains radioactive carbon 14 we get from the food we eat. It has a half-life of 5,730 years. And while it is natural, it is no less dangerous than man-made radioactivity.

The point is we are all constantly exposed to radiation of all sorts, including cosmic radiation and environmental radiation of varying degrees depending upon where we live and at what altitude. For example, if you live in Reno or Denver, given their altitudes, you are exposed to more cosmic radiation. Additionally, in Denver there is a further exposure to radiation from naturally occurring uranium in the area. I suppose if the folks in Denver were as proud of their high level of radiation as the folks in Leadville are of their lead, they might want to change Denver's name to Radiationville, Colorado, and then watch the exodus.

Americans have a fear of radiation far in excess of its actual danger. But we live with it every day, and at low levels it seems to be benign. In today's world it's important that we have an educated understanding of the nature of radiation and of its true threat rather than the one we all apparently imagine. Our educational institutions have not done well with this subject. In fact, most of us have never studied it at all. And it is greatly aggravated by the hyperbolic way it is presented by the media. Take, for example, the reporting on the meltdown at the Fukushima nuclear facility in Japan. It had been hit by a 50-foot wall of water from the 2011 Tōhoku earthquake and tsunami that destroyed many Japanese towns and villages and left 18,500 people dead or missing, most by drowning. The "Oh my God" over-the-top way the media has presented the meltdown would make you believe that it was a total disaster for human health and human life.

The United Nations Scientific Committee on the Effects of Atomic Radiation concluded that the radiation exposure following the nuclear accident at Fukushima did not cause any immediate health effects.[76] It also found that it was unlikely that any health effects would be attributed to it in the future among the general public or among the vast majority of workers. As of April 2, 2014, it stated that it had found no evidence to support the idea that the nuclear meltdown in 2011 would lead to an increase in cancer rates or birth defects. As of now there have been *no confirmed deaths* from radiation exposure at Fukushima. This comes as a great surprise to most Americans. I am at a total loss to understand why this has not been widely reported in the media. Might it be attributed to influence of the oil and coal industries?

Which brings me to the next point—global warming is upon us. Unless we reduce greenhouse gases (carbon dioxide) in the atmosphere, the future will be very grim indeed. Nuclear power is benign when it comes to greenhouse gas emissions. What a nuclear reactor does is heat water just like a coal plant.

The hot water turns to steam and the steam turns great turbines to produce electricity. The difference is that the coal plant emits carbon dioxide while the nuclear plant emits water vapor.

And there are plenty of statistics available showing the relative cost in human life depending on the type of facility used to generate electricity. It is measured in deaths per unit of electricity generated (terawatt hours). Here is a sampling:

- Coal, with 26% of the world's energy, kills 161 persons per terawatt hour;
- Oil, with 36% of the world's energy, kills 36 persons per terawatt hour;
- Wind, with less than 1% of the world's energy, kills 0.15 persons per terawatt hour;
- And nuclear, with 5.9% of the world's energy, kills 0.04 persons per terawatt hour.

So why isn't America busily building nuclear plants that are "green," safe, and efficient? Other than a rather generalized fear of radiation, the most common answer is nuclear waste.

A forgotten fact is that by the 1954 Atomic Energy Act, Congress encouraged public utilities to develop commercial nuclear power plants and limited their liability in the event of a nuclear accident. Meanwhile nothing had been done about the growing quantities of radioactive waste, so in 1982 Congress passed the Nuclear Waste Policy Act that laid out a plan with deadlines whereby the Federal Government would build one or more national waste repositories.[77] Whatever happened to that?

It turns out that nuclear waste is more of a political problem than a scientific or physical one. The concern with waste is centered on the fact that one of the by-products of nuclear power is plutonium, which has a half-life of 24,000 years and is widely (and erroneously) believed to be one of the most dangerous materials in the world. The prospect of storing plutonium, which will produce radiation for many thousands of years just scares politicians silly!

To understand nuclear waste it is helpful to review the process by which it is generated. In order to get a nuclear reaction that is hot enough to turn water into steam it's necessary to enrich uranium 238 by adding enough uranium 235 to achieve a self-sustaining nuclear fission reaction. In the reactor core the uranium 235 is depleted as some of its mass turns into energy (heat) following Einstein's equation $E=mc^2$.[78] Eventually it is depleted to the point where it is no longer able to sustain the chain reaction. The process leaves some uranium 238 and creates plutonium and many (so-called) fission fragments. The fission fragments are literally the broken remnants of the U-235 atom. Many are highly radioactive. Altogether this is what constitutes the nuclear waste we are concerned with. What do we do with it?

As mentioned, presently it is not politically possible to store it in its designated site, Yucca Mountain, Nevada. Rather, it is now left on-site at various nuclear power plants around the country in tanks that look like swimming pools that have marginal security and are possible targets for terrorists.

The solution is straightforward. The depleted uranium and the plutonium can be reprocessed, reconstituted and reused. This has been done now for many, many, years by the French who have 56 reactors producing 76% of their electricity. France successfully manages its radioactive waste with little fanfare in a densely-populated country slightly smaller in area than California and Nevada combined. Reusing the fuel completely removes the political bugaboo of storing the plutonium with its 24,000 year half-life and eliminates leaving the nuclear waste stored in rather unsecure swimming pools all over the country. Finally, it dramatically reduces the amount of waste to be stored. A large reactor can produce 25 to 30 tons of waste in any given year, almost all of which is the spent uranium and the plutonium. The remaining fission fragments, also called *fission products*, can be contained in a vitrified glass matrix and stored in stainless steel canisters underground in Yucca Mountain where they occupy no more than three cubic meters per reactor.

There are great misconceptions regarding radioactive waste management, the first being that spent fuel "must be safeguarded for millions of years." One hundred years is closer to the truth. Most of the fission products have short half-lives and decay away within a few years. Two of the most abundant fission products are strontium 90 and cesium 137. These isotopes have thirty-year half-lives and present the greatest public health risk. However, within a few hundred years they too decay away. It is not a thousand year storage problem as the newspapers would have you believe. These are the very procedures that the French have been successfully following for years. As for uranium, it has been stored in the ground around us for as long as the earth has existed, and obviously the human race has survived.

Nuclear power, based on any reasonable analysis, is very safe. And when compared to coal it is enormously safe. Moreover, we are now faced with global warming. Relying long-term on carbon-based energy production is totally unacceptable.

The Chernobyl disaster in 1986 and the Three-Mile Island accident both resulted from a loss of cooling, causing fuel meltdown and release of radioactive fission products. The consequences were quite different, however. In Chernobyl, the reactor *lacked the containment building* that is mandatory in modern western nuclear plants. Consequently, radioactivity was spread over a broad area, causing the evacuation of residents and closing an area within a 20-mile radius of the plant. This area is still closed and the residents have not returned.

At the Three-Mile Island accident in 1979, the containment building kept radioactivity from escaping, and the impact of the accident outside of the plant boundary was negligible. As a precautionary measure, residents living within a 20-mile radius of the plant were evacuated. They returned to their former homes within three weeks. Safety is possible with good design.

The World Health Organization in a 2005 statement titled *Chernobyl: The True Scale of the Accident* reported that a team of 100 experts in the field estimated that up to 4,000 from a population of over 600,000 people might ultimately die as a result of radiation exposure from the Chernobyl incident. While radiation spread over a broad area of eastern Europe, the resulting levels were quite low in most areas.

There are no 100%s in life. There are risks all around us. And while nuclear power is indeed very safe, nothing is risk-free. It is nevertheless a very important step towards avoiding a climate change disaster.

I would like to end this chapter on a personal note. On the Monday after Thanksgiving in 1957 I was sitting in my father's car in our driveway in Sacramento with a good college friend who had spent the holiday with my family. Since neither of us had a car we were waiting for my father to drive us back to college. The day was still quite dark and at exactly 6 A.M. the sky over Sacramento lit up like day and returned to dark in an instant. Neither of us had any idea what had just occurred.

We learned later that it was the atmospheric testing of an atomic bomb at the Yucca Flats proving ground in Nevada, some 300 miles from where we sat. Many of us do not know, and some of us who have been around for a while have forgotten, that the United States and the Soviet Union were at that time regularly conducting atmospheric atomic bomb tests. The one I have just described not only lit up Sacramento but it also lit up my curiosity about nuclear power which continues today. One of the most interesting aspects of the story is the fact that the college friend who was with me that morning, Craig Smith, went on to earn a Ph.D. in nuclear engineering and has led a very interesting life with projects all around the world since then. He remains a good friend and has been my mentor in writing this chapter and my critic for this book.

*"Haven't you anything non-military? Herbert is more interested
in the postwar world."*

Chapter 12

The Other 1%
(Or the Military Draft is the Test of a Just War)

The inscription over the rear entrance to the Memorial Amphitheater at Arlington National Cemetery reads:

DULCE ET DECORUM EST PRO PATRIA MORI
(It is sweet and fitting to die for your country.)

Really? I haven't heard that sentiment lately. To the contrary, wasn't it that thought that prompted us to dump the draft and hire The Other 1% to fight our wars for us?

Just mention bringing back the draft—and stand back. The immediate response—"Oh my God, my son, my daughter, my grandson, my granddaughter—they might get killed." Yes, indeed, that's a real test, isn't it? America's wars in the 20th century presented that question, each with a bit of a different twist.

WORLD WAR I

America has never wanted to get involved in European wars or power struggles. That certainly held true for World War I. Sending our boys off to die in a foreign war was a non-starter. It was going to take a draft to get them there.

The war began in August of 1914 and by 1916, when it was nearly two years old, Europe was self-destructing. The slaughter there and in the Mid-East was indescribable. Even so, America wanted none of it. The isolationism was so strong that President Wilson even ran his campaign that year with the slogan "He kept us out of war." However, after his reelection he went about enacting the draft: The Selective Service Act of 1917.

What did it take to get the Congress to enact the draft and send our boys off to die in Europe? Direct attacks on the U.S.—that's what! There was the sinking of five American ships with the loss of American lives plus the pledge of Germany to help Mexico reclaim Texas, New Mexico and Arizona. That finally did it. And given the millions upon millions of young men dying in the trenches, that was quite a commitment. There were over 36 million dead and wounded (16 million dead and 20 million wounded) by war's end. America had 116,000 dead and 204,000 wounded. Over one-half of the American dead were from disease, mainly the 1918 flu epidemic.

No doubt the American entry into the war helped bring it to an end, not only by its military personnel but also by its manufacturing base. America's ability to supply the allies was the death knell for Germany. America's delay saved American lives but prolonged the war.

It is very difficult to draft Americans to go abroad to die in what is seen as a foreign war. In WWI it took three years of carnage and *direct attacks* to get them there.

On a personal note, my father enlisted in January 1918, and

was a sergeant in the infantry stationed on Long Island, New York, waiting for the next troopship to take him to Europe when the Armistice was signed 11/11/11 (11 P.M. November 11, 1918). Lucky for him and lucky for me.

WORLD WAR II

The fight in America to keep it out of World War II was very strong and very bitter. For an in-depth account *Those Angry Days* by Lynne Olson is excellent.[79] The "America First Committee" movement had some surprising early supporters including Charles Lindbergh, the future president of Yale Kingman Brewster, and McGeorge Bundy who wrote on behalf of his Yale classmates that they "had deep-seated uncertainty about things for which they were willing to die." That is the question, isn't it?

Also, in the noninterventionist group: Future President Jack Kennedy, his future brother-in-law Sargent Shriver, future Justice of the Supreme Court Potter Stewart, future President Gerald Ford and a 15-year-old Gore Vidal. All eventually became interventionists.

In addition to the isolationist America First group there was also the problem that many in Congress had a deep-seated and bitter hatred of FDR. Sounds familiar.

The notion of a peacetime draft was unthinkable in America at the time. The most prestigious men and women in America were at loggerheads over the issue of going to war and of instituting the draft. The isolationists versus the interventionists. A committee of mothers hung interventionist Claude Pepper in effigy outside the Capitol Building. There was even a fistfight on the floor of the House. The problem was finally solved when President Roosevelt's opponent in the 1940 election, Wendell Willkie, endorsed the draft saying that it was the only democratic way to train for and secure our national defense. Oh, for the good old days of compromise. Finally, it took a direct attack on Pearl Harbor to get us into the war.

"Dulce et decorum est" made somewhat of a comeback

during World War II. Featured in this comeback were two prominent young men, Jack Kennedy and George Herbert Walker Bush. Neither of them ever needed to see combat. A phone call to Papa Prescott or Papa Joe would have landed them with nice desk jobs in Washington. Both of them went for combat in the Pacific Theater. That takes real guts. Their stories of heroism are well documented. Where are their military progeny today? Where are the men and women of the "Ivys" serving? Wall Street? Kennedy and Bush and hundreds of thousands of others passed the test. It was worth dying for.

Again, on a personal note, my closest friend as a youngster had her older brother killed in the war. He was a fighter pilot shot down over Belgium. His remains were only recently (within the last couple of years) located and brought home for burial. All the "boys" were in for the duration and it was a total commitment for everyone in America.

KOREAN WAR

When the Korean War broke out in mid-1950, the 1940 Draft Act was still in place. The war was conducted under a United Nations' mandate and was called a "Police Action." The purpose of the war was to contain communism. Communist North Korea had invaded the South at the height of the Red Scare in America. There was great anxiety about the intent of the Chinese and the Soviets and their support for North Korea. The United Nations forces, mainly American, were commanded by General Douglas MacArthur. The draft was still on.

The early stages of the war were a disaster for the American and United Nations forces. They were nearly driven off the end of the Korean Peninsula. The tide was turned by an invasion halfway up the peninsula at Inchon.

The war *never* had popular support in America.

In 1952 General Eisenhower was campaigning for the presidency and the war had ground to a standstill near the 38th Parallel where it had begun. At the time of his campaign the war had become so unpopular that Eisenhower made a now famous speech where he announced: "I shall go to Korea." He said that he would bring the war to an early and honorable end. He did. His effort resulted in a cease-fire that is still ongoing. No peace treaty. The war created 36,500 American deaths, 103,000 wounded and 8,000 MIA. It ended as a stalemate at the 38th Parallel. Can you sense the depth at which the American public wanted out of that war? *Its "boys" had been drafted to fight that war.* They did so honorably, but it ended in a draw!

Another personal note. My first cousin was drafted and shipped out just a few days before his wife gave birth to their first child. He is still missing in action these 60-plus years later.

VIETNAM WAR

For anyone who was an adult during the '60s and '70s just the mention of the Vietnam War brings to mind the civil unrest and riots that were ongoing as a result of the protests against the war in America. Draft cards were being burned. There were sit-ins, marches, and near riots, both on and off college campuses all across the country. The war, like Korea, was generated by the Cold War and the hope to contain the spread of communism. In July 1965 President Johnson turned it from support for South Vietnam into a full-fledged war by announcing the infusion of hundreds of thousands of American troops into the war. With the increase in American deaths and casualties, more and more attention was drawn to the nature of the war itself. Many believed it was a civil war in which we had no role, and there was a wholesale rejection of the draft going on across the country. Young men were simply refusing to serve. Others were moving to Canada to avoid going. Even those who weren't subject to the draft were in the streets and fomenting strife across the country. "Hell no, we won't go" was a chant across America. The 1968 Democratic Convention in Chicago was a major urban riot. The war dragged on for roughly ten years and ended mainly because America wanted out. 58,000 American soldiers died and 303,000 were injured. The draft killed the war.

THE DRAFT

I believe the Vietnam War was the cause of America abolishing the draft. I also think it was a terrible decision.

The draft is very important. It takes the temperature of America. Its abolition created *"The Other 1%,"* the small cadre of professional soldiers that we have fight our wars so that we can go shopping. It ended the test mentioned earlier by McGeorge Bundy: Is it something we would consider dying for? If the answer is no, why would you send someone else to do it?

There is another reason why the draft is important. When I was a youngster there were two ways that Americans were democratized—public schools and the draft. In my day the sons and daughters of lawyers and doctors went to public schools while the parochial schools were somewhat of a blue-collar experience. That has pretty well flipped over. The Catholic schools are now havens for the wealthy while the public schools are for the *hoi polloi*.

Likewise, the draft used to be a meeting place for a great cross-section of America. It, too, had a real democratizing effect. When I went through boot camp at Fort Ord, it seemed as though Hollywood had designed my company. We had ages ranging from 17 to 25 and included a deputy sheriff, Mormon missionaries, a disc jockey from Las Vegas, soon-to-be professional football players, lawyers, young men from every ethnic and racial group you can think of, some youngsters who were there as an election against going to jail, gays, college graduates and youngsters who had not finished high school, a policeman from San Francisco, teenage boys who had never had three meals a day before in their life, and a couple of guys who were just downright scary. By the time you got out, the company worked as a unit and you had made friends with folks that you would never have otherwise met. That is a good thing, too.

Another personal note. One of my closest friends in college, Earle Drake, after completing his military service, re-upped to go to Vietnam. After earning a Silver Star, he was killed in a tank accident while on maneuvers, leaving a wife and four children.

AFGHANISTAN AND IRAQ

When 9/11 happened, the military draft was a dim memory. We had long ago hired "The Other 1%" to fight our wars for us. But it was clear that the draft had shaped the wars of the 20th century. In World War I, when the slaughter in Europe and across the Mid-East was beyond imagination, it took direct attacks on the United States to get us to go to war. Likewise, in World War II, while Britain hung on for year after year of the Blitz, it wasn't until being attacked at Pearl Harbor that we joined the fight.

With the draft still in place, we went to war in Korea and Vietnam even though we hadn't been directly attacked. But as those wars dragged on and more and more American boys were drafted to go abroad and die, the hue and cry went up and caused the early termination of both of them. One was a draw, the other a loss.

The war in Afghanistan was something new. It began with tremendous support because it was launched to catch Osama bin Laden who had just attacked America. It caused a brief rebirth of *Dulce et decorum est.* Many young men and women volunteered to defend America.

Their enthusiasm might have been tempered a bit if they knew that the White House was already planning its war to depose Saddam Hussein in Iraq. They did not volunteer to fight that war.

The planning for Iraq began on January 30, 2001, just ten days after President George W. Bush's inauguration and seven months before 9/11. It began at a meeting of the National Security Council (NSC). In attendance were the President, Vice President Cheney, the Secretary of the Treasury Paul O'Neill, CIA Chief George Tenet, NSA Chief Condoleezza Rice, General Colin Powell, Secretary of Defense Donald Rumsfeld, Joint Chiefs Chairman Hugh Shelton, and Andy Card, White

House Chief of Staff.

According to O'Neill, the first item on the agenda was the Arab-Israeli conflict. It was the President's position that the conflict was a mess and the United States should disengage. The policy was that the combatants would have to work it out on their own.[80]

The next item on the agenda was Iraq. Thus, America was washing its hands of the conflict in Israel and was focusing on Iraq.[81] Getting Saddam Hussein was the administration's focus. The talk around the table was about how to remedy inadequate intelligence so as to discover Saddam's weapons program and to examine America's military options. This included how to use ground forces in the north and south of Iraq and how the armed forces could support groups inside the country to challenge Saddam.[82]

Just two days later the NSC met again, this time in the White House Situation Room. Again, the talk was about getting rid of Saddam. Rumsfeld asked the group to imagine what the region would look like without Saddam and with a regime that would be in line with U.S. interests.

According to O'Neill:

"From the start, we were building the case against Hussein and looking at how we could take him out and change Iraq into a new country. And if we did that it would solve everything. It was all about finding a way to do it. That was the tone of it. The President saying, *'Fine. Go find me a way to do this.'*"[83]

When you have decided to depose the leader of a sovereign country and are looking for excuses, whatever you come up with is purely pretextual, and certainly illegal.

The upshot of all of this is obvious. When 9/11 happened, the President and Ms. Rice weren't focused on the threats from Osama bin Laden but on figuring out a justification for attacking Iraq. Had they been paying attention to the warnings they were receiving about bin Laden, there may not have been a war in Afghanistan.

AFGHANISTAN

But there was. The campaign in Afghanistan began on October 7, 2001. Within two months it had met with great success. It swept the Taliban from power and ousted Al Qaeda from its safe haven. At the same time Hamid Karzai had been installed as the country's handpicked leader. By early December, Osama bin Laden had been chased into the caves of Tora Bora. His capture lay before them.

General Tommy Franks commanded the U.S. forces in Afghanistan. In his memoir Franks reported that on November 21 he got a call from Donald Rumsfeld advising him that the President wanted a war plan for Iraq. This was confirmed in Bob Woodward's book, *Plan of Attack,* where he reports that the President told Rumsfeld to get Franks to come up with such a plan. According to Franks he was then working on support for the Afghan units being assembled in the mountains surrounding Tora Bora. Frank's reaction to Rumsfeld's orders went this way: "Son of a bitch. No rest for the weary."[84]

So as The Other 1% was risking their lives to chase the world's most wanted criminal, the President of the United States, the Secretary of Defense and the commander of forces in Afghanistan were in the process of drawing up plans for invading Iraq!

Just as maddening, as bin Laden was trapped in Tora Bora, calls for American reinforcements were refused by Franks and Rumsfeld. They were relying instead on Afghan and Pakistani forces to make the catch.[85]

Really? Which country was attacked by bin Laden? And which country actually gave safe haven to Al Qaeda and bin Laden? Which country's troops were motivated to catch bin Laden? Which country had troops who sided with bin Laden? And what **KNUCKLEHEAD** would have reluctant Afghan rather than American troops go in for the kill?[86] Surprise. Surprise. Bin Laden escaped.

What then was left of the original U.S. mission? If we weren't going to chase bin Laden into Pakistan, isn't it "Mission Accomplished"? But be careful, there is always mission creep to create some back-fill. America supported the attack on Afghanistan to crush Al Qaeda and get bin Laden. Nation building wasn't on the program. Nevertheless, for the next dozen years we have stayed in Afghanistan as a nation-building exercise. How do you think the American public would have reacted if the troops that were being rotated into and out of Afghanistan for all those years were draftees from middle America and from the "Ivys" rather than The Other 1%? Reportedly, President Obama increased the troop level in Afghanistan by roughly 64,000 troops. If they were being supplied by the draft from various colleges and universities across the country would the nation have been so sanguine? If history is any lesson (refer to Korea and Vietnam), if the war in Afghanistan had been supplied by the draft it would have ended in about three years, not twelve.

IRAQ

After the January 30, 2001, meeting of the NSC, O'Neill received a memo from Rumsfeld that contained the following:

"The post-Cold War liberalization of trade in advanced technology goods and services has made it possible for the poorest nations on earth to rapidly acquire the most destructive military technology ever devised including nuclear, chemical, and biological weapons and their means of delivery. We cannot prevent them from doing so."[87]

The solution to this problem, which came out of these NSC meetings, was to depose Saddam:

"A weak but increasingly obstreperous Saddam might be useful as a demonstration model of America's new, unilateral resolve. If it could effectively be shown that he possessed, or was trying to build, weapons of mass destruction (WMDs)—creating an 'asymmetric threat,' in the neoconservative parlance, to U.S, power in the region— his overthrow would help 'dissuade' other countries from doing the same. At least, that seemed to be the idea."

To this the President responded:

"Fine. Go find me a way to do this."[88]

That was "why" we went to war in Iraq. It is unbelievable that we began an offensive war, for pretextual reasons in order to intimidate other small countries from getting WMDs.

This was confirmed by President Bush in a press conference he gave in March 2002.[89] The President first responded to a question concerning the development of low yield nuclear weapons that could be used against "China, Iran, Iraq, Libya, North Korea, Russia, and Syria." He said that this was standard policy because the nuclear arsenal is for deterrence. The follow-up question was, "Why a policy that might go after a country like Libya or Syria?" The President's answer? "First of all, we've got all options on the table because we want to make it very clear to nations that you will not threaten the United States or use weapons of mass destruction against us, or our allies or friends." The President's response is just a paraphrase of the quote above as reported by Paul O'Neill.

Turn then to the time when the administration announced that Saddam had WMDs and that we were going to invade Iraq. Suppose that the military force to be used was to be staffed by a universal draft of American youngsters. Based on recent history it would clearly be a no-go. We had not been attacked nor had any of our allies nor anyone else, for that matter. Furthermore, the sons and daughters of America would be demanding actual proof that there was a threat at hand. They would have surfaced the article written by George H.W. Bush and Brent Scowcroft in March 1998 outlining all the reasons why Saddam should not be removed, including the potential breakup of Iraq. Brutal dictators are brutal in order to hold their countries together. Remove the dictator and you open Pandora's box with possible civil war or a failed state. As the Bush/Scowcroft article stated: If they had removed Saddam in 1991, "We would have been forced to occupy Baghdad and, in effect, rule Iraq.... Had we gone the invasion route, the U.S. could conceivably still be an occupying power in a bitterly hostile land."[90] With the draft in place, would there have been minor riots on various college campuses around the country?

Likely.

Former NSC Chief Scowcroft followed up with another article (August 2002) where he again pointed out all the reasons not to invade Iraq: Scant evidence tying Saddam to terrorist organizations and even less evidence tying him to 9/11. There was also little evidence to indicate that the United States was a target of any of his aggressions. He concludes that an invasion of Iraq would result in a military campaign very likely to be followed by a large-scale, long-term military occupation.[91]

None of this got much mention in the popular press that had knuckled under to White House rhetoric. For the first time in history in a situation where we had not been attacked, where our allies had not been attacked, where no one had been attacked, where there was no actual proof of aggression towards the United States or of the possession of weapons of mass destruction and with cogent arguments being made by those in a position to know, the American public said, "Oh what the hell, our kids aren't going, let's leave it up to The Other 1%." Polls showed that 70% of Americans said that since they did not have any dog in the fight, let's go to war.

CONCLUSION

If the Iraq war depended upon a universal draft it would not have happened. Incredibly the media and the Congress knuckled under to the jingoism of the White House. During the war most of America was on total disconnect. No talk around the water cooler, as they say. Few people knew anyone in The Other 1%. The actual cost of the war was kept "off book" by the White House. Pictures of the young men and women killed in the battle for Iraq, coming home through Dover Air Force Base, were not allowed. If we weren't willing to die for our country, how could we simply turn it over to The Other 1%?

There is an interesting almost poetic parallel between the efficacy of having a drafted army and the "just war,"[92] and that is the defensive war against an armed attack. The draft works well in that circumstance, as demonstrated by World War I and

World War II, although it is best to have it in place far ahead of the actual attack! The more removed from a defensive war, the more problematic the draft will be (as in Korea and Vietnam). Finally, when there is no attack and no draft and you are the aggressor, you likely fall into the category of illegal warfare as we did when we invaded Iraq, in complete contravention of American values and policy.

Dulce et Decorum Est[93]

Bent double, like old beggars under sacks,
Knock-kneed, coughing like hags, we cursed through sludge,
Till on the haunting flares we turned our backs,
And towards our distant rest began to trudge.
Men marched asleep. Many had lost their boots,
But limped on, blood-shod. All went lame; all blind;
Drunk with fatigue; deaf even to the hoots
Of gas-shells dropping softly behind.

Gas! GAS! Quick, boys!—An ecstasy of fumbling
Fitting the clumsy helmets just in time,
But someone still was yelling out and stumbling
And flound'ring like a man in fire or lime.—
Dim through the misty panes and thick green light,
As under a green sea, I saw him drowning.

In all my dreams before my helpless sight,
He plunges at me, guttering, choking, drowning.

If in some smothering dreams, you too could pace
Behind the wagon that we flung him in,
And watch the white eyes writhing in his face,
His hanging face, like a devil's sick of sin;
If you could hear, at every jolt, the blood
Come gargling from the froth-corrupted lungs,
Obscene as cancer, bitter as the cud
Of vile, incurable sores on innocent tongues,—
My friend, you would not tell with such high zest
To children ardent for some desperate glory,
The old lie: *Dulce et decorum est*
Pro Patria mori.

—**Wilfred Owen**

When will we learn? Old men declare wars that young men
have to fight.

* * *

"No, no, Senator, no thanks are necessary at this time."

Chapter 13

Hindsight is 20/20
(Is it Really?)

As we try to explain away our mistakes we frequently justify ourselves by saying, "Oh well, hindsight is 20/20" without recognizing that the phrase is meant to be ironic. Taken as a truism it tends to make your mistake look less egregious.

It is Monday morning quarterbacking. Had the quarterback done "this" we would have won the game without recognizing that had we done "this" the other team might've done "that." With hindsight we can pick whatever facts we like while ignoring the ones that are less helpful.

Take Pearl Harbor, for example. It was a grievous error committed by the Roosevelt administration that had adequate warnings. Throughout 1941 FDR was continuously urged by his advisors to get engaged in the War. In May 1941, he spoke to the nation and proclaimed a state of "unlimited national emergency," vowing full-scale support for Great Britain. Just two weeks later a German submarine sank an American freighter, the *SS Robin Moor*, in the south Atlantic. Still FDR stayed out of the war. In October, one of our destroyers, the *USS Kearney* (DD-432), was struck by a German torpedo and America lost eleven sailors with many more injured, although the *Kearney* did not sink. At the same time, FDR told Churchill that he was just looking for an incident to justify opening hostilities. Yet he did nothing. Finally, at the end of October another of our destroyers, the *USS Reuben James* (DD-245), was sunk with the loss of 115 members of its crew. Again the President elected not to enter the war. There was enormous pressure on FDR to get in the war coming from all sides, long before Pearl Harbor.[94]

By then, it was a foregone conclusion that we were going to have to join the Allies to defeat the Axis. It was a mistake, a grave mistake, for the President to wait for a calamity before doing what needed to be done. Well, it came. It was Pearl Harbor and we lost 2,400 men plus many of the warships of our fleet.

It has been said, in hindsight, at least Pearl Harbor finally got us in the war—as if that in some way justifies what happened there. It does not. It was and remains a serious mistake to have waited for a catastrophe to get the United States involved. Hindsight justifies nothing.

It is why historians so often disagree. They have many facts to choose from to get to whatever preordained idea or conclusion they are promoting. So picking a fact from the past in an attempt to make your error more understandable or less problematic should get you nowhere. Properly understood, the phrase is simply ironic, meaning that you should not try to ameliorate what you did by claiming that there was something obvious that justified your mistake. Yes?

Acknowledgements and Credits

I am grateful to the following publishers for permission to reproduce material: New Directions Publishing Corporation, for the poem *Dulce et Decorum Est,* by Wilfred Owen, from THE COLLECTED POEMS OF WILFRED OWEN, copyright ©1963 by Chatto & Windus, Ltd. Reprinted by permission of New Directions Publishing Corp. Also, my sincere thanks to Condé Nast for permission to reproduce the following cartoons that originally appeared in the *New Yorker* magazine:

1. Cover and frontispiece, George Price 9/14/46 "Whoa Damn it, whoa…"
2. p. viii Mick Stevens 3/13/89 "The Stat Family"
3. p. 10 Robert J. Day 12/29/62 "Shouldn't there only be 9 of us up here?"
4. p. 36 Alain 2/20/43 "Still, did you ever stop to think where you and I would be if it weren't for evil?"
5. p. 44 Joseph Mirachi 10/24/64 "This toy is designed to hasten the child's adjustment to the world around him. No matter how carefully he puts it together, it won't work."
6. p. 46 Joseph Mirachi 9/26/88 "The poor are getting poorer, but with the rich getting richer it all averages out in the long run."
7. p. 52 Joseph Mirachi 12/31/74 "Do you ever have one of those days when everything seems un-Constitutional?"
8. p. 72 J. B. Handelsman 8/7/95 "You've been around here longer that I have. What are 'congressional ethics'?"
9. p. 74 J. B. Handelsman 5/29/89 "How very exciting! I have never before met a Second Amendment lawyer."
10. p. 98 Whitney Darrow Jr. 12/9/44 "Haven't you anything non-military? Herbert is more interested in the postwar world."

11. p. 112 Charles Barsotti 7/4/88 "No, no senator, no thanks are necessary at this time."
These eleven cartoons are © Condé Nast.

Thanks also to the Tee and Charles Addams Foundation for permission to reproduce the Charles Addams cartoon on page. 22 ("Mountain Pass") that originally appeared in the New Yorker Magazine on 2/25/60. © 1950 Charles Addams.

The cherry tree sketch on page 31 courtesy of Nancy J. Smith.

My thanks first to my wife Barbara for her ideas, her editing, her patience and her support. Next thanks to my wonderful publishers Nancy and Craig Smith, for their direction, encouragement, book design, and helping me structure my essays, and without whom this book would not be possible. My thanks also to my friends who have taken the time to read all or part of my book and for their encouragement and critiques that have been invaluable. This is not to say that any or all of them agreed with any or all of what I have to say since it was my intent in writing these essays to promote and provoke thought: Jim Randlett; Cecilia Delury; Rosemary Kelley; Richard Thompson; Neal Brockmeyer; John Bond; Mike Hackard; Joel Carey; Dennis Mangers; Karen Skelton; Hon. Frank Damrell, ret.; Chuck Post; Hon. Ron Tochterman, ret.; Hon. Rick Sims, ret.; Brian Landsberg; Msgr. Jim Kidder; Steven Felderstein; Hon. Thadd Blizzard; Malcolm Weintraub and Geoff Burroughs.

End Notes

[1] Durant, Will and Ariel. (1961). p. 173 *The Story of Civilization: Part vii, The Age of Reason Begins.* New York: Simon and Schuster.

[2] Ibid., p. 174

[3] Barzun, Jacques. (2000). *From Dawn to Decadence.* New York: Harper Collins.

[4] Translation: *The Reality, Vaccines, and the Appearance of Reality.*

[5] Barzun, op. cit., p. 204

[6] Durant, op. cit., p. 175

[7] Durant, loc. cit.

[8] Gould, Steven Jay. (1995) p. 48. *Dinosaur in a Haystack: Reflections in Natural History.* New York: Harmony Books.

[9] Roe v. Wade 410U.S.113 was a historic decision about abortion rights. See note 21.

[10] Brown v. Board of Education,347 U.S. 483 (1954)

[11] Plessy v. Ferguson,163 U.S.537 (1896)

[12] Kennedy, David M. (1999). pp. 325-335. *Freedom from Fear: The American People in Depression and War, 1929-1945.* Oxford: Oxford University Press.

[13] Wesberry v. Sanders,376 U.S.1 (1964)

[14] Reynolds v. Sims,377 U.S. 533 (1964)

[15] As noted in Chapter 10, the original intent of the Bill of Rights was to restrict the powers of the Federal Government *vis à vis* the States.

[16] Citizens United v. Federal Election Commission ,558 U.S. 310 (2010)

[17] McCutcheon v. FEC,572 U.S. ___ (2014)

[18] Marbury v. Madison, 5 U.S. 137 (1803)

[19] Burke, Edmund (1775) "Speech on the Conciliation with

America."
[20] *Bible* Mathew 19:24
[21] Note: For a full description of U.S. Supreme Court legal cases cited in this book, access https://supreme.justicia.com/cases/federal/us/410/113. The last two numbers (410/113) are the case numbers for the case in question, in this example, Roe v. Wade. Roe v. Wade (410/113: 1973) was a history-making decision regarding the right of women to have an abortion. In the Court's mind, the decision hinged on the Due Process Clause of the 14th amendment.
[22] See generally Wood, Gordon. (2009). Chapters 1 and 2 in *Empire of Liberty—a History of the Early Republic 1789-1815*. Oxford: Oxford University Press.
[23] James Srodes Review, (September 29, 2009), *Washington Times*: Washington D.C.
[24] Wood, op. cit., pp. 8-9, 34, 302 and 542.
[25] U.S. Constitution, Article I, Section 3; Article II, Section 1; 12th Amendment.
[26] Wood, op. cit., pp. 209-10.
[27] Wood, op. cit., pp. 69-72.
[28] Barron v. Baltimore, 32 U.S. 243 (1833).
[29] Wood, op. cit. pp. 19-24, 84, 121.
[30] U.S. Constitution, Article IV, Section 4.
[31] Brown v. Board of Education, 347 U.S. 483 (1954).
[32] Weinberger v. Wiesenfeld, 420 U.S. 636, 638 fn. 2 (1975). Mapp v. Ohio, 367 U.S. 643 (1961).
[33] Quincy Railroad v. Chicago, 166 U.S. 226 (1897).
[34] Reynolds v. Sims, 377 U.S. 533 (1964).
[35] Wesberry v. Sanders, 376 U.S. 1 (1964).
[36] Wang, Sam *New York Times*, February 3, 2013, p. SR1.
[37] Wood, op. cit., pp. 19-21.
[38] Wesberry, op. cit., p. 13.
[39] Oxford English Dictionary (OED). (2000). vol. v, p 906.Oxford: Oxford University Press
[40] Bush v Gore, 531 U.S. 98 (2000). See p. 104.

[41] Wood, op. cit., pp. 209-10.
[42] Wang, *loc. cit.*
[43] The District of Columbia v. Heller, 554 U.S. 570 (2008).
[44] United States v. Miller, 307 U.S. 174 (1939)
[45] The District of Columbia v. Heller, op. cit., pp.54-56
[46] Scalia, Antonin. (1997). *A Matter of Interpretation.* Princeton NJ: Princeton University Press
[47] Ibid., p. 16.
[48] Scalia, op. cit., p. 18.
[49] Scalia, op. cit., p. 22.
[50] Scalia, op. cit., p. 23.
[51] McCulloch v. Maryland, 17 U.S. 316 (1819).
[52] Scalia, op. cit., p. 37.
[53] Scalia, op. cit., p. 37.
[54] Scalia, op. cit., p. 38.
[55] Barron v Baltimore, 32 U.S. 243 (1833).
[56] Ibid., p. 247.
[57] Barron, op. cit., pp. 250-251.
[58] Barron, op. cit., p. 247.
[59] Wood, Gordon S. (2009). pp. 65-72 *Empire of Liberty,* Oxford: Oxford University Press.
[60] Ibid., p. 72.
[61] Oxford English Dictionary (OED). (2000). Vol. i, p. 634. Oxford: Oxford University Press.
[62] Heller, op. cit., Fn. 3. p. 6: "And Justice Stevens is dead wrong to think. . ."
[63] Scalia, op. cit., p. 43.
[64] Scalia, op. cit., p. 47.
[65] Heller, op. cit., p. 3.
[66] Heller, op. cit., p. 12.
[67] Heller, op. cit., p. 15.
[68] Heller, op. cit., p. 18.
[69] Heller, op. cit., p. 56.
[70] Scalia, op. cit., p. 43.
[71] Scalia, op. cit., p. 22.

[72] <u>McDonald v. Chicago</u>, 571 U.S. 742 (2010).

[73] Scalia, op. cit., pp. 24-25.

[74] Scalia, op. cit., p. 143.

[75] McDonald, op. cit., Scalia concurring, p.1

[76] United Nations Scientific Committee on the Effects of Atomic Radiation. (2014). p. 10-11. *UNSCEAR 2013 Report: Vol 1. Report to the General Assembly. Scientific Annex A: Levels and effects of radiation exposure due to the nuclear accident after the great east-Japan earthquake and tsunami.* New York: United Nations.

[77] The Nuclear Waste policy Act of 1982 (42USC 10222). This Act establishes both the Federal Government's responsibility to provide a place for the permanent disposal of high-level radioactive waste and spent nuclear fuel, and the generators' responsibility to bear the costs of permanent disposal.

[78] Upon fissioning, Uranium 235 loses 8 units of mass to become Strontium 90 and Cesium 137. The atomic weight mass balance is 235 minus (90+137) equals 8. The lost mass has been converted into energy (heat and radiation). This is one of the most common results of fission. Other combinations of fission products are possible.

[79] Olson, Lynn. (2013). *Those Angry Days: Roosevelt, Lindbergh, and America's Fight Over WWII*, 1939-41. NY: Random House.

[80] Suskind, Ron. (2004). p. 71-72. *The Price of Loyalty. (George Bush, the White House, and the Education of Paul O'Neill*) New York: Simon and Schuster.

[81] Ibid., p.74.

[82] Ibid., p.75.

[83] Ibid., p.86.

[84] Kerry, Senator John, Chairman. (2009). p. 12. *Tora Bora Revisited: How We Failed To Get bin Laden and Why It Matters Today;* (A report to members of the Committee on Foreign Relations, United States Senate). Senate print 111-35. Washington D.C.: U.S. Government Printing Office.

[85] Ibid., p.2.

[86] Kerry, op. cit., p.13.

[87] Suskind, op. cit., p.77.

[88] Suskind, op. cit., p. 86.

[89] Presidential News Conference, March 13, 2002.

[90] Bush, George Sr. and Scowcroft, Brent. (March 2, 1988). "Why we didn't remove Saddam." *Time Magazine.*

[91] Scowcroft, Brent, (August 15, 2002). "Don't Attack Saddam." *Wall Street Journal.*

[92] See in general: St. Augustine, (5th century A.D. *City of God,* and St. Thomas Aquinas, (1275) *Summa Theologica, part II, Ethics.*

[93] Owen, Wilfred, (1964) p. 55 "Dulce et Decorum Est," in *The Collected Poems of Wilfred Owen,* New York: New Directions Publishing Corporation. Copyright 1963 by Chatto & Windus, Ltd. Reprinted with permission.

[94] Olson, op. cit., Chapter 25.

REVIEWS

Regarding *N is for Knuckleheads*: I couldn't put it down! Joe Genshlea is a great storyteller and I found this series of short essays thoroughly fascinating and thought provoking. Many of us have progressive ideas and opinions that we share all too frequently without benefit of fact checking and research. Joe Genshlea has obviously taken considerable time to make sure his opinions are supported by facts and shares them in an historical context that provides what the old radio personality Paul Harvey used to refer to as "the rest of the story". I plan to buy multiple copies of this book to share with family and friends, both socially progressive and conservative. It is sure to spawn some very interesting conversations.
--**Dennis Mangers**, Former California State Assemblyman

N is for Knuckleheads: I liked it a bunch. Thought provoking; made you think; excellent information; I learned things I should have known.
--**Jim Randlett**, Randlett•Nelson•Madden, Government Relations

I liked *"Knuckleheads"*! I find myself going to sleep and waking up thinking about, agreeing with, or debating your various observations and conclusions. What more could you ask from a book designed to "provoke, stimulate, and educate?" Any thinking person (and some others as well) will enjoy the book immensely and find themselves rereading sections from time to time as new thoughts occur. The book clearly demonstrates why you are such a successful trial lawyer. You do have a "Point of View," and that is what makes the book so interesting and readable.
--**Richard Thompson,** President, Caterpillar Diesel Engines (Retired)

Made in the USA
San Bernardino, CA
24 February 2016